REGENTS RESTORATION DRAMA SERIES

General Editor: John Loftis

THE TRAGEDY OF JANE SHORE

NICHOLAS ROWE

The Tragedy of Jane Shore

Edited by

HARRY WILLIAM PEDICORD

UNIVERSITY OF NEBRASKA PRESS · LINCOLN

Publishers on the Plains

UNP

Regents Restoration Drama Series

The Regents Restoration Drama Series provides soundly edited texts, in modern spelling, of the more significant plays of the late seventeenth and early eighteenth centuries. The word "Restoration" is here used ambiguously and must be explained. A strict definition of the word is unacceptable to everyone, for it would exclude, among many other plays, those of Congreve. If to the historian it refers to the period between 1660 and 1685 (or 1688), it has long been used by the student of drama in default of a more precise term to refer to plays belonging to the dramatic tradition established in the 1660s, weakening after 1700, and displaced in the 1730s. It is in this extended sense—imprecise though justified by academic custom—that the word is used in this series, which includes plays first produced between 1660 and 1737. Although these limiting dates are determined by political events, the return of Charles II (and the removal of prohibitions against operation of theaters) and the passage of Walpole's Stage Licensing Act, they enclose a period of dramatic history having a coherence of its own in the establishment, development, and disintegration of a tradition.

The editors have planned the series with attention to the projected dimensions of the completed whole, a representative collection of Restoration drama providing a record of artistic achievement and providing also a record of the deepest concerns of three generations of Englishmen. And thus it contains deservedly famous plays—*The Country Wife, The Man of Mode,* and *The Way of the World*—and also significant but little known plays, *The Virtuoso,* for example, and *City Politiques,* the former a satirical review of scientific investigation in the early years of the Royal Society, the latter an equally satirical review of politics at the time of the Popish Plot. If the volumes of famous plays finally achieve the larger circulation, the other volumes may conceivably have the greater utility, in making available texts otherwise difficult of access with the editorial apparatus needed to make them intelligible.

The editors have had the instructive example of the parallel and senior project, the Regents Renaissance Drama Series; they have in fact used the editorial policies developed for the earlier plays as their own, modifying them as appropriate for the later period and as the experience of successive editions suggested. The introductions to the separate Restoration plays differ considerably in their nature. Although a uniform body of relevant information is presented in each of them, no attempt has been made to impose a pattern of interpretation. Emphasis in the introductions has necessarily varied with the nature of the plays and inevitably—we think desirably—with the special interests and aptitudes of the different editors.

Each text in the series is based on a fresh collation of the seventeenth- and eighteenth-century editions that might be presumed to have authority. The textual notes, which appear above the rule at the bottom of each page, record all substantive departures from the edition used as the copy-text. Variant substantive readings among contemporary editions are listed there as well. Editions later than the eighteenth century are referred to in the textual notes only when an emendation originating in some one of them is received into the text. Variants of accidentals (spelling, punctuation, capitalization) are not recorded in the notes except in instances in which they have, or may have, substantive relevance. Contracted forms of characters' names are silently expanded in speech prefixes and stage directions and, in the case of speech prefixes, are regularized. Additions to the stage directions of the copy-text are enclosed in brackets.

Spelling has been modernized along consciously conservative lines, but within the limits of a modernized text the linguistic quality of the original has been carefully preserved. Contracted preterites have regularly been expanded. Punctuation has been brought into accord with modern practices. The objective has been to achieve a balance between the pointing of the old editions and a system of punctuation which, without overloading the text with exclamation marks, semicolons, and dashes, will make the often loosely flowing verse and prose of the original syntactically intelligible to the modern reader. Dashes are regularly used only to indicate interrupted speeches, or shifts of address within a single speech.

Explanatory notes, chiefly concerned with glossing obsolete

words and phrases, are printed below the textual notes at the bottom of each page. References to stage directions in the notes follow the admirable system of the Revels editions, whereby stage directions are keyed, decimally, to the line of the text before or after which they occur. Thus, a note on 0.2 has reference to the second line of the stage direction at the beginning of the scene in question. A note on 115.1 has reference to the first line of the stage direction following line 115 of the text of the relevant scene. Speech prefixes, and any stage directions attached to them, are keyed to the first line of accompanying dialogue.

JOHN LOFTIS

Stanford University

Contents

List of Abbreviations

Authorized Editions

Q   First edition, 4to, Bernard Lintot, 1714
D2   Second edition, 12mo, Bernard Lintot, 1714

Unauthorized Editions ⏤

Op S. Powell for P. Cambel, 8vo, Dublin, 1714
Sp T. Johnson, 16mo, The Hague, 1714

Introduction

The Tragedy of Jane Shore was first acted at the Theatre Royal in Drury Lane on February 2, 1714, and was an immediate success. Two editions of the play appeared within the year. Rights had been sold to Bernard Lintot, who announced the first edition on January 28;[1] a second edition soon followed. These were the only authorized editions published during the author's lifetime, and collation of them with the various "Third Editions" printed for Lintot in 1719, 1720, and 1723 reveals no further revision. This would appear consistent with Dr. Johnson's comment some sixty years later upon Rowe's habits of writing: "Being by a competent fortune exempted from any necessity of combating his inclination he never wrote in distress, and therefore does not appear to have ever written in haste. His works were finished to his own approbation, and bear few marks of negligence or hurry."[2] It can be assumed that Rowe would have been equally careful in revisions and corrections.

However, apparently unauthorized editions of the tragedy were sold in Dublin and at The Hague in 1714. These piracies—an octavo edition, S. Powell for P. Cambel, Dublin (Op), and the notorious T. Johnson, The Hague, a sextuodecimo (Sp)—were based upon Lintot's first edition (Q). Although nothing is unusual about the Dublin edition, Johnson's Hague edition omits the Drury Lane actors' names from the Dramatis Personae, drops two lines (ll. 64–65) in Act IV, and, most important, includes the two brief passages in Act III suppressed at the time the drama was licensed for production. The Lord Chamberlain had cancelled a line and a half (ll. 173–74) from Hastings' speech to Gloster concerning "meddling priests":

> As if they feared their trade were at an end
> If laymen should agree.

[1]*The Post Boy*, January 26–28, 1714. Lintot advertised the drama and proposed to print "a small number . . . on fine paper. . . . No more being to be thus printed than are bespoke."

[2]Samuel Johnson, *The Lives of the English Poets*, ed. George Birkbeck Hill (Oxford, 1905), II, 70.

Whatever the fifteenth-century reference, the Lord Chamberlain was sensitive to political overtones in the eighteenth century; the lines only too clearly hinted at contemporary Whig clergy's insistence on absolving their countrymen from the oath of loyalty to James II and his son. The same delicacy caused cancellation of two lines in Gloster's reply (ll. 184–85); the passage pointed too broadly to the Succession Act which barred the Stuarts from the English throne:

GLOSTER.

    What, if the same estates, the Lords and Commons,
      Should alter—

HASTINGS.   What?

GLOSTER.   The order of succession?

The two passages also appear in *Poems on Various Occasions, by Nicholas Rowe,* 1714, printed by Edmund Curll as the final lines in the collection and entitled "The Exceptionable Passages left out in the Acting and Printing of the Tragedy of Jane Shore." Curll's claim would appear to be substantiated by the fact that T. Johnson took care to set the two passages in italics in his Hague edition. They are now generally accepted as of Rowe's own composition.[3]

The Tragedy of Jane Shore has been edited three times previously in the present century. Sophia Chantal Hart in 1907 and James R. Sutherland in 1929 used the first edition (Q) as the basis for their texts;[4] George H. Nettleton and Arthur E. Case in 1939 used the corrected second edition (D2).[5] The present edition is based once again upon the first edition. The few differences between the second edition and the first—and indeed those between the two unauthorized editions, either unnoticed or neglected by previous editors—are negligible and serve only to point

---

[3]*British Dramatists from Dryden to Sheridan,* ed. George H. Nettleton and Arthur E. Case, rev. George Winchester Stone, Jr. (New York, 1969), p. 927. Previous editors have supplied the original lines from Curll's edition. It is a question as to whether Johnson took the lines from that work or whether Curll took them from the Hague edition. I am inclined to the former theory.

[4]Hart, *The Fair Penitent* and *Jane Shore* (Boston, 1907); Sutherland, *Three Plays by Nicholas Rowe* (London, 1929).

[5]*British Dramatists from Dryden to Sheridan,* pp. 501–25.

up the careful attention and correction exercised by the author or the copy-reader when the manuscript frist arrived at the printer's shop. Punctuation, capitalization, and spelling have been modernized in this edition except in those instances where antique forms have been retained to comply with Rowe's versification.

The historical Jane Shore was married when quite young to a goldsmith named William Shore (sometimes called Matthew), an affluent citizen of London. To his misfortune his beautiful young wife captured the affections of his king, Edward IV, who quickly established her in a royal dwelling. All this had been related in *The History of King Richard III* (ca. 1513) by Sir Thomas More, who was at great pains to sing the lady's praises for her devotion to the downtrodden and her generosity to every unfortunate. But misery set in upon the death of Edward IV, and Jane Shore, now a mistress of Lord Hastings (according to More's account), fell under the displeasure of the Protector, the future Richard III. Hunted and persecuted following Hastings's execution, she came to a miserable end as a beggar in the streets of London.

Jane Shore was also memorialized by Thomas Churchyard, whose sentimental *Complaint of Shore's Wife* is one of the better contributions to the second edition of the *Mirror for Magistrates* (1563), by Michael Drayton in *An Epistle of Mistress Shore to King Edward the Fourth* (1597–1602), and others. She is either mentioned or appears as a character in *The True Tragedie of Richard III* (1594, a "contention play"), in Shakespeare's *Richard III* (1592–93), and in *King Edward IV*, Parts I and II (1599), frequently attributed at least in part to Thomas Heywood, and earlier attributed entirely to him.

All of these derive from More's history, which was the basis of John Hardying's *Metrical Chronicle* (1543). In 1548 Edward Hall adapted the Hardying version in his *Chronicle*, which in turn was later adapted by Raphael Holinshed in his *Chronicle* (1577); Shakespeare's *Richard III* is based upon Holinshed. Since many of Nicholas Rowe's characters in *The Tragedy of Jane Shore* appear also in Shakespeare—Gloster, Lord Hastings, Buckingham, Ratcliffe, Catesby, Derby, and the Bishop of Ely—one might assume that Rowe in his celebrated "Imitation of Shakespeare" merely rewrote the play from the point of view of his heroine. Yet such an impression would be misleading; though Rowe obviously relied on Shakespeare for the Gloster-Hastings material in the earlier part of his drama,[6] it is *Edward IV*, Part II, that is the prime source of his domestic plot.

Earlier critics have noted Rowe's indebtedness to that play, though with varying degrees of emphasis. Sophia Chantal Hart, in her 1907 edition, mentions both Shakespeare's *Richard III* and the anonymous *True Tragedie of Richard III* as sources and points out that *Edward IV* "has more material similar to Rowe's than either of [them] or Sir Thomas More's account." She adds, however, that the two plays, *Edward IV* and *Jane Shore*, "are as unlike in details of treatment as Rowe's style is unlike Shakespeare's style, which he avowedly professed to imitate."[7]

James R. Sutherland, in his 1929 edition, states that Rowe's sources are obvious: Sir Thomas More and Shakespeare's *Richard III*, "most notably from Act III, Sc iv." He notes, however, that the catalogue of Rowe's library mentions a volume of plays by Heywood and suggests that there are hints of *Edward IV* in Rowe's play, especially in the later scenes.[8]

I am convinced that Rowe not only possessed the plays of Heywood but that he had studied and thoroughly mastered *Edward IV*, Part II. None of the other sources on the life of Jane Shore, from Sir Thomas More to the early street ballads, convey even a hint of the disguise plot found in *Edward IV*—the husband's return from the Continent as Flud-Shore (Rowe's Dumont-Shore); the ballad tells us of Shore only that "from England then he goes away/ To end his life beyond the sea."[9] There are close resemblances between Rowe's fictitious Bellmour and two characters in the earlier play: Sir Robert Brackenbury, and Young Aire, who was executed for assisting Jane Shore. In general, however, Rowe's characters are less down-to-earth. For example, the Mistress Blague of *Edward IV*, to whom Jane delivers her goods for safekeeping and by whom she is later rejected, is an earthy pragmatist, involved in no romantic plot; when she turns Jane out of her house, she says, "I love you well, but love

[6]See Appendix B.
[7]*The Fair Penitent* and *Jane Shore*, p. xxiv.
[8]*Three Plays by Nicholas Rowe*, pp. 347–48.
[9]See Appendix B, ll. 57–58.

myself better."[10] Rowe's far more refined Alicia is driven only by jealousy.[11]

Such a change is an indication of what Rowe was about in adapting the story to eighteenth-century purposes. He was returning to the methods he had used in adapting Massinger's *The Fatal Dowry* as *The Fair Penitent* (1703), compressing a sprawling canvas of action and dialogue into a well-articulated frame determined by the dramatic rules of his age. Gone are the heady actions, the battle scenes, the on-stage executions, all the violence Elizabethan audiences admired; they are replaced with set-pieces of narrative and with pathetic episodes. Likewise, thought sequences gleaned from *Edward IV* are altered and elaborated to fit Rowe's design. In *Edward IV* Mistress Blague rejects Jane thus:

> 'Twas never other like but that such like filthiness
> Would have a foul and detestable end,

and Jane replies:

> Time was that you did tell me otherwise,
> And studied how to set a gloss on that,
> Which now you say is ugly and deformed.[12]

Rowe adds sentimental pathos to Jane's reproach in his parallel scene:

> And yet there was a time when my Alicia
> Had thought unhappy Shore her dearest blessing,
> And mourned the livelong day she passed without me;
> When paired like turtles, we were still together;
> When often as we prattled arm in arm,
> Inclining fondly to me, she has sworn
> She loved me more than all the world beside.
>   (V.203–209)

Longer speeches in *Edward IV* might well have been the inspiration for Rowe's, as in these lines spoken by Jane in Part II.

> Farewell unto you both! and London too!

. . . .

[10]*The Dramatic Works of Thomas Heywood*, ed. R. H. Shepherd, 6 vols. (London, 1874), I, 159. I have modernized spelling and typography in all quotations from this edition.

[11]Sir Thomas More describes Mistress Blague as a "lace-seller" to the court; Heywood endows her with ten thousands pounds; and Rowe elevates her to "noble birth," fit for a liason with Lord Hastings.

[12]*Works of Thomas Heywood*, I, 160.

All things that breathe, in their extremity,
Have some recourse of succour. Thou hast none.
The child offended flies unto the mother,
The soldier struck retires unto his captain,
The fish, distressed, slides into the river,
Birds of the air do fly unto their dams,
And underneath their wings are quickly shrouded,
Nay, beat the spaniel and his master moans him.
But I have neither where to shroud myself,
Nor any one to make my moan unto.[13]

These lines serve as the character's expression of her immediate feelings. In Rowe their counterpart becomes an observer's reflection, a set piece—Dumont-Shore's apostrophe to an Augustan peace at the close of Act II:

O lady!—but I must not, cannot tell you
How anxious I have been for all your dangers,
And how my heart rejoices at your safety.
So when the spring renews the flow'ry field,
And warns the pregnant nightingale to build,
She seeks the safest shelter of the wood,
Where she may trust her little tuneful brood,
Where no rude swains her shady cell may know,
No serpents climb, nor blasting winds may blow;
Fond of the chosen place, she views it o'er,
Sits there and wanders through the grove no more.
Warbling she charms it each returning night,
And loves it with a mother's dear delight.
(II.331–343)

Jane Shore had many things in its favor prior to its first public performance. First of all, the professionals at Drury Lane were delighted to find a new script calling for an evenly balanced cast of principals and based upon an ancient royal scandal. And publishers and booksellers rallied to their opportunity; a reading public already familiar with the lady's pathetic story through the ancient street ballads[14] was showered with hastily printed "lives" of Jane Shore. Typical is one with the title *The Life and Character*

[13]Ibid., pp. 165–166.
[14]See Appendix B.

of Jane Shore Collected from our best Historians, Chiefly from the Writings of Sir Thomas More: Who was her contemporary, and personally knew her. No less than five printers and booksellers had banded together to publish it.[15] Edmund Curll joined the rush with his *Memoirs of the Lives of King Edward IV and Jane Shore, Extracted from the best Historians.*[16] These and others achieved second and even third editions prior to the opening night of Rowe's tragedy. And once the drama had been launched successfully, many of these pamphlets gained in popularity.

The cast of the first performance and the eighteen other performances that season was the finest in the Drury Lane roster. Ann Oldfield, the Marcia in Joseph Addison's *Cato* the previous season, played Jane Shore, and Mary Porter, famous for her Belvidera in Otway's *Venice Preserved,* played her friend Alicia. Cibber appeared as Gloster, Barton Booth as Lord Hastings, and Robert Wilks, third member of the Triumvirate, as Dumont, the disguised William Shore. The supporting cast was made up of the best of the older actors, among them Mills, Husband, and Bowman.

Jane Shore became a staple in the repertory and remained so throughout the century—and not at the patent houses only. When Henry Giffard and his wife played at Odell's theatre in Ayliffe Street, Goodman's Fields, in the season of 1729–30, Mrs. Giffard excelled as Jane Shore. The couple kept this drama in repertory for eight more seasons after they opened their New Theatre in Goodman's Fields in 1732–33. Meanwhile, the company at Covent Garden began playing the tragedy in the season 1734–35. In the famous season of 1746–47 when the public flocked to Covent Garden to view the old and the new, James Quin and young David Garrick, with Ryan, Mrs. Pritchard, and Mrs. Cibber, *Jane Shore* achieved a run of nine consecutive nights (and three more nights in the season). The following season at Drury Lane, now with Garrick as joint manager, most of these actors were on hand to play another run of seven nights (and

[15]*"Printed and sold by J. Brown at the Black Swan without Temple-Bar, W. Taylor at the Ship in Paternoster Row, N. Cliffe in Cheapside, J. Morphew near Stationers-Hall, and A. Dodd at the Peacock without Temple-Bar. 1714. Price Six Pence."*

[16]*"Printed for E. Curll, at the Dial and Bible against St. Dunstan's Church in Fleetstreet. 1714. Price 6d."*

two more before the season's end), with Delane replacing Quin as Gloster and young Spranger Barry replacing Ryan as Dumont-Shore.

Jane Shore proved the most popular of Rowe's "she-tragedies," holding its place in the repertory well into the nineteenth century. Among other great actresses to appear in the drama were Mrs. Woffington, Mrs. Yates, Mrs. Siddons, Fanny Kemble, and (in the twentieth century) Genevieve Ward as Jane Shore, and Mrs. Bellamy, Mrs. Barry, and Miss Younge as Alicia. Male stars included such names as John Henderson and William Powell (both protegés of Garrick), and John Phillip Kemble.

The companies had reason enough to delight in *Jane Shore.* All actors are prone to value the number of lines in their roles, and eighteenth-century actors were quick to recognize such a well-wrought, well-balanced work. An analysis of the acting parts shows that Rowe provided not one but two pairs of leading roles, almost equal in length and importance. Jane Shore as heroine has some 440 lines to Lord Hastings's 356; Gloster, around whom so much of the action turns, has 317 lines to Alicia's 299, while the Dumont-Shore role trails with 245. Yet the Dumont-Shore character has a long, pathetic scene with his dying wife in the final act. That *Jane Shore* delighted not only the actors but the audiences is suggested by George Winchester Stone, Jr.'s comment in *The London Stage:* ". . . by the end of the century it had had 381 performances, 10 of which were 'By Command,' 72 of which were for benefits, and 47 of which were called for 'At the Desire of Several Persons [often Ladies] of Quality.' "[17]

The success of *Jane Shore* was of vital importance to Rowe because he had had three successive failures previously. He had begun a youthful career with three highly successful plays—*The Ambitious Stepmother, Tamerlane,* and *The Fair Penitent* were all produced in his twenties—he had experienced three failures in succession, *The Biter* (1704), *Ulysses* (1705), and *The Royal Convert* (1707).[18] Could it be that he was "written out"? What more could he do? He knew his craft; and in all his plays he had followed

---

[17]*British Dramatists from Dryden to Sheridan,* p. 501.

[18]*The Biter* was damned in its first performance. *Ulysses* had an unspectacular run of nine performances and was repeated once later in the season. It was not a real success. *The Royal Convert* achieved only seven performances in all.

the lines of evolution that led through Lee, Banks, and Otway, who, after the ultimate collapse of heroic drama, had established the "she-tragedy" in a special atmosphere of the strongest pathos. Had he not produced for his own century a new and significant kind of tragedy, more "regular" and decorous, sweeter in numbers? Axalla and Selima in *Tamerlane* had evoked an audience's pity to the point of challenging interest in that drama's overriding theme of (Whig) liberty; Rowe had moved on to give that same audience Calista and Lothario in *The Fair Penitent*. Perhaps his critics had been correct in pointing out that Lothario was so daringly drawn as to overbalance the tragedy. Yet Calista, despite her moral ambiguities, was a technical triumph suiting Rowe's own pathetic mood. And Lothario had written his name into the language. Rowe was a devout believer in the pseudo-classical rules; he knew he possessed the skill to develop "regular" plots and to give his stage a diction, a "poetic coloring," supremely pathetic but acceptable as "natural" to his audience. What more?

In any event, after the failure of *The Royal Convert*, November 25, 1707, Rowe withdrew from the competition and soon announced his intention of editing Shakespeare. His *Works of Mr. William Shakespear* appeared in six volumes in 1709, in seven volumes in 1710. Not until four years later was Rowe to venture upon a new tragedy, *Jane Shore*. He was then forty years old and presumably at the height of his powers; he was acclaimed as editor of Shakespeare; he had made use of a vacation from playwrighting. Now in Jane Shore he had found a heroine celebrated by ballads, historians, and Shakespeare, and this time without the traits of character which had limited the pathetic appeal of Calista in *The Fair Penitent* and Ethelinda in *The Royal Convert*. Had *Jane Shore* failed, Rowe might have considered that this was an end to the matter. But the play was an enormous success. And Rowe had made his comeback with what he proudly insisted was a tragedy "Written in Imitation of Shakespear's Style."

Despite the resounding success of *Jane Shore* in performance, Rowe's contemporaries lost no time in attacking him for his presumption in regard to Shakespeare. Swift and Pope were reluctant to accept his claim. Swift sneered as he wrote, "I have seen a play professedly writ in the style of Shakespeare, wherein the resemblance lay in one single line, 'And so good morrow t'ye, good master lieutenant.' "[19] And Pope complained privately to Joseph Spence that "it was mighty simple in Rowe, to write a play now, professedly in Shakespeare's style, that is, professedly in the style of a bad age."[20] Charles Gildon published a pamphlet in the form of a tavern symposium titled *A New Rehearsal, or Bays the Younger*,[21] in which he deplored not only *Jane Shore* but all of Rowe's plays. The subject under discussion is the imitation of Shakespeare's style:

DAPPER.

   . . . I warrant you don't admire the Stile.

FREEMAN.

   I speak for my part that I do not, 'tis a sort of *Motley, Linsey Woolsey* Stile, Gloster has, by his *Holydame,* and St. *Paul,* and many of *Shakespear's* Words, but the rest speak generally in the Stile of the Moderns.

DAPPER.

   Why, I believe the Poet design'd that, for he has directed the Dress of *Gloster* and *Jane* to be of those Days; but those of all the other Players to be Modern.

TRUEMAN.

   I think it so far from a recommendation, that it is written in the Stile of *Shakespear,* that it ought to damn it; . . . the best Stile, is that which arrives to the Perfection of the Language than in Being, such as is that of *Cato,* which is the best Standard of Dramatic Diction which we have in our Tongue.[22]

Thomas Dibdin quotes an anonymous theatrical writer of Gildon's time[23] to answer the criticism rather lamely: "With all its merit . . . and the hold it has taken of the public, this play has

[19]Motte's *Miscellanies 1727,* "The Last Volume," p. 41. Swift not only misquotes the line but places it in the wrong play; the line is from Rowe's *Lady Jane Grey.* See Edna Leake Steeves, ed., *The Art of Sinking in Poetry* (New York, 1952), p. 145.

[20]*Anecdotes, Observations, and Characters of Books and Men,* ed. J. M. Osborn (Oxford, 1966), I, 183.

[21]"Printed for J. Roberts in Warwick-Lane (London, 1714)."

[22]*A New Rehearsal,* p. 77.

[23]*The London Theatre* (London, 1815), Vol. VI.

been the subject of perpetual criticism, and some strictures on it breathe more a spirit of envy than of candour."

Most of these early critics failed to see why a scattering of oaths and archaic phrases and timid paraphrases of better-known Shakespearean lines should warrant Rowe's effrontery in comparing his work to that of Shakespeare. Samuel Johnson provides a summary of the century's judgment on the subject: "In what he thought himself an imitator of Shakespeare it is not easy to conceive. The numbers, the diction, the sentiments, and the conduct, every thing in which imitation can consist, are remote in the utmost degree from the manner of Shakespeare; whose dramas it resembles only as it is an English story, and as some of the persons have their names in history."[24]

In our century Sophia Chantal Hart approached such a claim with skepticism: "The reader of *Jane Shore* wonders how an editor of Shakespeare could fancy this play bore any resemblance to the work of the great dramatist. Evidently in the eighteenth century there was no very clear conception, even by those who valued him most, of what Shakespeare stood for."[25] But she shrewdly suggested: "We shall have a truer measuring-rod for Rowe's 'Imitation' of Shakespeare, if we observe the treatment Shakespeare's plays received at the hands of literary men of that day. It serves better than anything else can to show the gulf that divides the sixteenth from the late seventeenth and the eighteenth centuries—the change of mood in English drama."[26] Yet Sutherland defends Rowe's claim as an imitator of Shakespeare, explaining it this way: "Critics have all along been prone to deny that Rowe's play contains the least trace of Shakespeare. . . . But *Jane Shore* is obviously written in a style unfamiliar to playgoers of the second decade of the eighteenth century, and that style is so clearly pseudo-Shakespearean, that Rowe's claim cannot be disputed. The most casual examination of his plays must reveal to any competent critic frequent echoes and parodies of Shakespeare's voice."[27] Sutherland substantiates his argument with numerous and significant quotations.

It would appear that both of these modern editors are in some

[24]*Lives of the English Poets*, II, 69.
[25]*The Fair Penitent* and *Jane Shore*, p. xxviii.
[26]Ibid., p. xxxiii.
[27]*Three Plays by Nicholas Rowe*, p. 33.

measure correct, Hart with her "measuring-rod" and Sutherland with his "echoes and parodies." Perhaps the question is best resolved by what must unfortunately be an overlong reference to an anonymous critic of Rowe's own time who produced in 1714 "A Review of *The Tragedy of Jane Shore*, Consisting of Observations on the Characters, Manners, Stile, and Sentiments."[28]

After chiding fellow critics for being over-zealous in the matter of the three unities, terming them "niceties of pure mechanism," he remarks on the suitability of the characters in the tragedy for moral instruction, especially Jane Shore, an adulteress with an otherwise "clear and unspotted reputation." Then the writer continues:

> Now it is fit we consider the Style and Sentiments of this play; the first is professedly in *Shakespear's* Manner, and the second seems not an Imitation of any particular way of Thinking among our great Poets. I distinguish here between the Style, and the Thought, because it is evident that the Author has not thought it proper to give a loose to his Fancy, and spring out into *Shakespear's* ungovernable Flights; nor has he indeed brought in his Images so thick as that Poet spun out his Metaphors, or struck into any of his uncommon and peculiar Ways of Thinking.
>
> The Style then in this place is no more than the Phrase, the manner of Expression, which is indeed like *Shakespear's* in all the Parts of it that deserve Imitation. . . . I would not intimate that *Shakespear* is not followed by this Author, but only say that the Phrase[s], rather than the Sentiments, are what seem to be the Subject of the perfect Imitation. . . . For all the Rust and Obsoleteness of *Shakespear* is filed off and polished, what is rough, uncouth, and ill-fashioned in his Expression, is left behind, and so much only remains of him as is agreeable to the Ear, significant or venerable. . . . Now this sort of Imitation has its Difficulties, for it must be a long and familiar Acquaintance with an Author to make such an apt Resemblance of his Manner, as not to appear like a scrupulous Servility to him, nor too remote a Likeness which requires Times to suit the Copy with the Original. . . . it is what Sir *John Denham* says of Mr. *Cowley* in his imitating the Ancients, *wearing their Dress, and not their Cloaths;* the

[28]"Printed for J. Roberts, in Warwick-Lane, 1714. (Price Six-pence)."

one were a Robbery, the other shews a Value and Respect to the Owner.[29]

In imitating Shakespeare's style and at the same time "regularizing" his own tragedy according to contemporary standards, Rowe had to cut away not only "Rust and Obsoleteness" but Shakespeare's "ungovernable Flights" of imagery. He preserved the phrase, the "manner" of Shakespeare's expression, rather than sentiments which could not be his own. He simplified his figures in order to indulge his own particular genius, what he termed "poetic coloring" and what Thomas Gray was to call "Mr. Rowe's flowers of eloquence."

One further comment upon Rowe's style: the failure of *The Royal Convert* appears to have been deserved, but in it Rowe had created in the Christian Ethelinda a distinctive character. Sutherland calls attention to Rowe's shrewd but half-apologetic lines in the Epilogue:

> To some, I know, it may appear but oddly,
> That this Place, of all others, should turn godly.[30]

It is not surprising that in his next play Rowe should carry his Christian sentiments further. Jane's first words as she enters to speak with her neightbor Bellmour are a sharp reminder to the audience of spiritual obligations.

> How few, like thee, enquire the wretched out,
> And court the offices of soft humanity;
> Like thee, reserve their raiment for the naked,
> Reach out their bread to feed the crying orphan,
> Or mix their pitying tears with those that weep!
>
> (I.ii. 12–16)

In the concluding act, as Jane returns from the scene of public penance, weary and starving, she addresses her fate with a mosaic of paraphrases from at least six books of the Old Testament and two of the New Testament.[31] All of this is surely in character for a heroine newly come from a public cross, and yet it enhances the pathetic and "complaining" spirit Rowe devised for his public. In his final drama, *Lady Jane Grey* (Drury Lane, 1714–15), the

---

[29] Ibid., pp. 10–13.
[30] *Three Plays by Nicholas Rowe*, p. 32.
[31] I Kings, Psalms, Proverbs, Isaiah, Ezekiel, Hosea, Luke, Revelation.

new approach by way of religious sentiment is again apparent. But this time scriptural paraphrase is more subtly handled; it seems almost hidden beneath the virulence of a Protestant sermonizing, at the close of which the heroine chooses death rather than apostasy.

Again we are indebted to Rowe's anonymous contemporary, the author of "A Review of *The Tragedy of Jane Shore, etc.*," who suggests that this is a

> Particular, almost peculiar to this Writer, and [one] which gives no inconsiderable Grace and Ornament to his Compositions. This is an Allusion very frequent with him to Passages in Holy Writ, sometimes the Places are but lightly touched upon; at others we may observe many Lines and elegant Descriptions transplanted into his Writings, and the Phrase itself preserved with a becoming Dignity, and much to the Embellishment of the Poetry ... such Allusions are not only pardonable, but deserve our Applause.

He points out that "the Books, then, from whence most of the Images and noble Ideas are drawn, are those which many have supposed to have been writ Originally in Verse, such as Job, the Psalms, and many of the Prophets."[32] The writer believes all this influenced Rowe's style because the scriptures abound with boldness of metaphor couched in an "Harmonious Numerosity" little inferior to verse itself. He poses the question: why should not "a Christian Poet take advantage of these materials which may very much heighten and improve his own?"[33]

As the inheritor of the "she-tragedy" from the seventeenth century, Rowe mastered the form and made it new and significant for his age. And in Jane Shore he found a suitable heroine for the evocation of pity. Nor is Jane Shore alone in her complaints and misfortunes. Each of the principal characters has his own private cause for lamentation and proclaims it upon every appearance. Lord Hastings, troubled about the State and the aim of the Protector, is harrassed by a jealous mistress; he is a loyal subject about to be cut off from the living. The jealous Alicia betrays, is betrayed, loses her lover and brings about his death, and is left as forlorn as her rival. The patient Dumont-Shore

[32]"A Review of *The Tragedy of Jane Shore*," p. 10.
[33]Ibid., pp. 10–11.

must view the woes of an unfaithful wife he has already forgiven; should he rescue her he would endanger his own life. Even the colorless Bellmour, through whom the audience is brought to sympathize with both husband and wife, suffers from an excessive compassion for the victims of an arbitrary villain.

Richard Cumberland, in 1817, complained that Rowe's plot was well-chosen but "not always well-managed." He smiled at the firm friendship pledged by Alicia to Jane Shore which changes almost immediately into implacable hatred, a change Rowe never bothers to explain. He complained of the "trick beneath the dignity of tragedy," the sleight-of-hand changing of Jane's petition to the Protector, a "maneuver barely passable in a comedy." At times Cumberland referred not to the architecture of the drama but rather to the absurdities exhibited by characters swollen with the sentimental: Lord Hastings, for example, after describing himself as a partiot, shows himself capable of base ingratitude and the actions of a cowardly bully in his attack upon both Jane Shore and Dumont. And yet even Cumberland was forced to admit the power of the great scenes between Gloster and Jane Shore, between Hastings and Alicia. He attributed the popularity of *Jane Shore* in his day to what he called "Versification, wrought up to its highest polish."[34]

And in this he provided an explanation for the success of *Jane Shore*. Rowe's reputation was based upon the fact that he could write speeches for the actors of his day. They were the instruments by which he charmed the audience with a new style and diction.

HARRY WILLIAM PEDICORD

Thiel College

---

[34]"Critique of *Jane Shore*," *British Drama* (London, 1817), I, ix.

THE TRAGEDY OF JANE SHORE

—————Coniunx ubi pristinus illi
Respondet curis.
　　　　　　　—Virgil *Aeneid* 6.473–74

Coniunx . . . curis] ". . . where her first husband . . ./ understands her
unhappiness" (trans. C. Day Lewis [Oxford, 1952]).

2

To His Grace the Duke of Queensberry and Dover, Marquis of Beverley, &c.

My Lord,

I have long lain under the greatest obligations to Your Grace's family, and nothing has been more in my wishes than that I might be able to discharge some part, at least, of so large a debt. But your noble birth and fortune, the power, number, and goodness of 5 those friends you have already, have placed you in such an independency on the rest of the world that the services I am able to render to Your Grace can never be advantageous, I am sure not necessary, to you in any part of your life. However, the next piece of gratitude, 10 and the only one I am capable of, is the acknowledgment of what I owe: and as this is the most public, and indeed the only way I have of doing it, Your Grace will pardon me if I take this opportunity to let the world know the duty and honor I had for your illustrious 15 father. It is, I must confess, a very tender point to touch upon; and at the first sight may seem an ill-chosen compliment, to renew the memory of such a loss, especially to a dispostion so sweet and gentle, and to a heart so sensible of filial piety as Your Grace's has been, even 20 from your earliest childhood. But perhaps this is one of those griefs by which the heart may be made better; and if remembrance of his death bring heaviness along with it, the honor that is paid to his memory by all good men shall wipe away those tears, and the 25

9. sure not] sure, not *Q, D2, Op.*
Sp does not print the Dedicatory Epistle.

0.1. *The Duke . . . &c.*] Charles Douglas (1698–1778), third Duke, created Earl of Solway in 1706, Lord Justice General from 1763 to his death.

15–16. *your illustrious father*] James Douglas (1662–1711), the second Duke, created Duke of Dover and Marquess of Beverley in 1708, appointed third Secretary of State in 1709.

3

example of his life set before your eyes shall be the
greatest advantage to Your Grace in the conduct and
future disposition of your own.

In a character so amiable as that of the Duke of
Queensberry was, there can be no part so proper to   30
begin with as that which was in him, and is in all good
men, the foundation of all other virtues, either religious or civil; I mean good nature—good nature, which
is friendship between man and man, good breeding
in courts, charity in religion, and the true spring of   35
all beneficence in general. This was a quality he possessed in as great a measure as any gentleman I ever
had the honor to know. It was this natural sweetness
of temper which made him the best man in the world
to live with, in any kind of relation. It was this made   40
him a good master to his servants, a good friend to
his friends, and the tenderest father to his children.
For the last, I can have no better voucher than Your
Grace; and for the rest I may appeal to all that have
had the honor to know him. There was a spirit and   45
pleasure in his conversation, which always enlivened
the company he was in, which, together with a certain
easiness and frankness in his disposition, that did not
at all derogate from the dignity of his birth and character, rendered him infinitely agreeable. And as no man   50
had a more delicate taste of natural wit, his conversa-
tions always abounded in good humor.

For those parts of his character which related to the
public, as he was a nobleman of the first rank, and
a minister of state, they will be best known by the great   55
employments he passed through, all which he dis-
charged worthily as to himself, justly to the princes who
employed him, and advantageously for his country.
There is no occasion to enumerate his several employments, as Secretary of State, for Scotland in particular,   60
for Britain in general, or Lord High Commissioner of
Scotland, which last office he bore more than once;

---

62. *which . . . once*] in 1700 and again in 1706. In 1703 Queensberry was
deprived of office for association with the Jacobites; he was restored to
office in 1706.

but at no time more honorably, and (as I hope) more
happily, both for the present age and for posterity,
than when he laid the foundation for the British Union.   65
The constancy and address which he manifested on
that occasion are still fresh in every body's memory,
and perhaps when our children shall reap those
benefits from that work which some people do not
foresee and hope for now, they may remember the   70
Duke of Queensberry with that gratitude which such
a piece of service done to his country deserves.

He showed upon all occasions a strict and immediate
attachment to the crown, in the legal service of which
no man could exert himself more dutifully nor more   75
strenuously. And at the same time no man gave more
bold and generous evidences of the love he bore to
his country. Of the latter, there can be no better proof
than the share he had in the late happy Revolution;
nor of the former than that dutiful respect and   80
unshaken fidelity which he preserved for Her present
Majesty, even to his last moments.

With so many good and great qualities, it is not at
all strange that he possessed so large a share, as he
was known to have, in the esteem of the Queen and   85
her immediate predecessor; nor that those great
princes should repose the highest confidence in him:
and at the same time, what a pattern has he left behind
him for the nobility in general, and for Your Grace
in particular, to copy after.   90

Your Grace will forgive me, if my zeal for your wel-
fare and honor (which nobody has more at heart than
myself) shall press you with some more than ordinary
warmth to the imitation of your noble father's virtues.
You have, my Lord, many great advantages which may   95

---

65. *foundation . . . Union*] As royal commissioner he carried through
the treaty for the union of England and Scotland in 1707.

66–67. *manifested on that occasion*] See Defoe's "History of the Union"
for a characterization of the second Duke of Queensberry.

75–76. *more dutifully nor more strenuously*] despite threats of bodily harm
and even assassination.

79. *late happy Revolution*] the Bloodless Revolution of 1688.

encourage you to go on in pursuit of this reputation;
it has pleased God to give you naturally that sweetness
of temper which, as I have before hinted, is the foundation of all good inclinations. You have the honor to
be born not only of the greatest, but of the best of 100
parents; of a gentleman generally beloved, and generally lamented; and of a lady adorned with all virtues
that enter into the character of a good wife, an admirable friend, and a most indulgent mother. The natural
advantages of your mind have been cultivated by the 105
most proper arts and manners of education. You have
the care of many noble friends, and especially of an
excellent uncle, to watch over you in the tenderness
of your youth. You set out amongst the first of mankind, and I doubt not but your virtues will be equal 110
to the dignity of your rank.

That I may live to see Your Grace eminent for the
love of your country, for your service and duty to your
prince, and, in convenient time, adorned with all the
honors that have ever been conferred upon your noble 115
family; that you may be distinguished to posterity, as
the bravest, greatest, and best man of the age you live
in, is the hearty wish, and prayer of

My Lord,
Your Grace's most obedient, and 120
most faithful, humble servant,
N. ROWE

107–108. *an excellent uncle*] William Douglas, first Earl of March, second
son of the first Duke of Queensberry.

Dramatis Personae

Men

DUKE OF GLOSTER	*Mr. Cibber*
LORD HASTINGS	*Mr. Booth*
CATESBY	*Mr. Husbands*
SIR RICHARD RATCLIFFE	*Mr. Bowman*
BELLMOUR	*Mr. Mills* 5
DUMONT	*Mr. Wilks*
[EARL OF DERBY]	[Unknown]
[BISHOP OF ELY]	[Unknown]
[DUKE OF BUCKINGHAM]	[Unknown]

Women

ALICIA	*Mrs. Porter* 10
JANE SHORE	*Mrs. Oldfield*

SEVERAL LORDS OF THE COUNCIL, GUARDS, AND ATTENDANTS

Scene: *London*

---

1. *Duke of Gloster*] or Duke of Gloucester, afterwards King Richard III (1452–85).

1. *Mr. Cibber*] Colley Cibber (1671–1757), actor, dramatist, poet laureate; one of the triumvirate managing Drury Lane Theatre in Rowe's lifetime.

2. *Lord Hastings*] William Hastings (ca. 1430–83), master of the Mint and chamberlain of the royal household under Edward IV.

2. *Mr. Booth*] Barton Booth (1681–1733), another manager of Drury Lane, who established himself as a tragic actor as Pyrrhus in Ambrose Phillips's *The Distressed Mother* (1712).

3. *Catesby*] William Catesby, one of Richard III's chief advisors, not to be confused with Sir William Catesby, the later Catholic recusant.

3. *Mr. Husbands*] The name may be a mispelling for Benjamin Husband (fl. early eighteenth century). "Husbands" is on the roster at Lincoln's Inn Fields with Betterton in 1700–1702, at Drury Lane 1702–4, and again at Lincoln's Inn Fields 1705–6. Husband acted at Drury Lane 1706–9, and at the Queen's Theatre and Greenwich; from 1710–11 on, as "Husband," he is a permanent member of the Drury Lane Company.

4. *Sir Richard Ratcliffe*] or Radcliffe (d. 1485), another advisor to Richard III. He carried out the execution of Earl Rivers, Richard Grey, Thomas Vaughan, and Sir Richard Haute. He was made a Knight of the Garter and High Sheriff of Westmoreland for life by Richard III.

4. *Mr. Bowman*] John Bowman (1664–1739), actor and singer, member of Betterton's company, came to Drury Lane 1710–11.

5. *Mr. Mills*] John Mills (d. 1736), a strong romantic actor in roles

7

ranging from Macbeth, Bajazet, and Chamont to Falstaff in both parts of Shakespeare's *Henry IV*.

6. *Dumont*] assumed name of William Shore, goldsmith.

6. *Mr. Wilks*] Robert Wilks (1665–1732), third member of the triumvirate, noted for his acting of Sir Harry Wildair in Farquhar's *The Constant Couple* (1699) and of Hamlet in Shakespeare's play.

7. *Earl of Derby*] Thomas Stanley, first Earl of Derby (ca. 1435–1504). Edward IV made him steward of the household and Richard III made him constable of England. His appearance as the Earl of Derby in Rowe's tragedy is an anachronism: Stanley was created Earl of Derby by Henry VII *after* the death of Richard III.

8. *Biship of Ely*] John Morton became Bishop of Ely in 1479, encouraged Buckingham's defection from Richard III, and upon the death of Richard became a chief counselor to Henry VII.

9. *Duke of Buckingham*] Henry Stafford, second duke of Buckingham (1454?–1483), married to Catherine Woodville, sister of Edward IV's queen. He assisted Richard III in the arrest of Rivers, Grey, and young Edward V and persuaded the public of the illegtimacy of the heirs of Edward IV. He defected to Richmond's party, was betrayed by one of his own men, and was executed at Richard's order.

10. *Mrs. Porter*] Mary Porter (d. 1765), a pupil of Betterton, famous for her Belvidera in Otway's *Venice Preserved*. Her first appearance was at Lincoln's Inn Fields (1699) and her last at Covent Garden (1742).

11. *Mrs. Oldfield*] Anne Oldfield (1683–1730) created such different roles as Lady Betty Modish in Cibber's *The Careless Husband* (1704), Sylvia in Farquhar's *The Recruiting Officer* (1706), and Marcia in Addison's *Cato* (1713).

PROLOGUE
Spoken by Mr. Wilks

Tonight, if you have brought your good old taste,
We'll treat you with a downright English feast—
A tale which, told long since in homely wise,
Hath never failed of melting gentle eyes.
Let no nice sir despise our hapless dame   5
Because recording ballads chant her name:
Those venerable ancient song-enditers
Soared many a pitch above our modern writers:
They caterwauled in no romantic ditty,
Sighing for Phillis's, or Chloe's pity.   10
Justly they drew the fair, and spoke her plain,
And sung her by her Christian name—'twas Jane.
Our numbers may be more refined than those,
But what we've gained in verse, we've lost in prose.
Their words no shuffling, double-meaning knew,   15
Their speech was homely, but their hearts were true.
In such an age, immortal Shakespeare wrote,
By no quaint rules nor hampering critics taught;
With rough, majestic force he moved the heart,
And strength and nature made amends for art.   20
Our humble author does his steps pursue;
He owns he had the mighty bard in view,
And in these scenes has made it more his care
To rouse the passions than to charm the ear.
Yet for those gentle beaux who love the chime,   25

4. Hath] *D2, Sp;* have *Q, Op.*

---

6. *recording ballads*] e.g., *Shore's Wife*, 1593; *A New Ballad of King Edward and Jane Shore*, 1671; *The Woeful Lamentation of Jane Shore*, n.d.; *The Unfortunate Concubines, Fair Rosamond and Jane Shore*, 1708.

7. *song-enditers*] song writers.

9. *caterwauled*] screeched like tomcats.

10. *Phillis, or Chloe's pity*] Phillis, a country girl in the 3rd and 5th *Eclogues* of Virgil: Chloe, shepherdess beloved by Daphnis in the pastoral romance by Longus, *Daphnis and Chloe*.

13. *numbers*] verses.

15. *shuffling*] deceitful.

22.] referring to the title-page statement, "Written in Imitation of Shakespear's Style."

9

The ends of acts still jingle into rhyme.
The ladies, too, he hopes, will not complain;
Here are some subjects for a softer strain—
A nymph forsaken, and a perjured swain.
What most he fears is, lest the dames should frown,   30
The dames of wit and pleasure about town,
To see our picture drawn unlike their own.
But lest that error should provoke to fury
The hospitable hundreds of Old Drury,
He bid me say, in our Jane Shore's defense,   35
She doled about the charitable pence,
Built hospitals, turned saint, and died long since.
For her example, whatsoe'er we make it,
They have their choice to let alone or take it:
Though few, as I conceive, will think it meet   40
To weep so sorely for a sin so sweet;
Or mourn and mortify the pleasant sense,
To rise in tragedy two ages hence.

---

34. *hospitable hundreds*] The playhouse designed by Sir Christopher Wren and erected in 1674 had a capacity of approximately one thousand spectators and remained unaltered until 1747.

The Tragedy of Jane Shore

Written in Imitation of Shakespeare's Style

ACT I

[I.i]   *Scene, the Tower.*
Enter the Duke of Gloster, Sir Richard Ratcliffe, *and* Catesby.

GLOSTER.

>   Thus far success attends upon our councils,
>   And each event has answered to my wish;
>   The queen and all her upstart race are quelled;
>   Dorset is banished, and her brother Rivers
>   Ere this lies shorter by the head at Pomfret.   5
>   The nobles have with joint concurrence named me
>   Protector of the realm. My brother's children,
>   Young Edward and the little York, are lodged
>   Here, safe within the Tower. How say you, sirs,
>   Does not this business wear a lucky face?   10
>   The scepter and the golden wreath of royalty

---

1. *councils*] council meetings.
3. *the queen . . . race*] the Woodville family. Elizabeth, widow of Sir John Gray of Groby, had married Edward IV secretly. Her father, Sir Richard Woodville, Lord Rivers, had been made Edward's treasurer. He was later executed by Warwick at Kenilworth in 1469. Her brother, Anthony, the next Lord Rivers, was made guardian and protector of Edward, Prince of Wales.
4. *Dorset . . . and her brother Rivers*] Thomas, Marquis of Dorset, Edward IV's wife's son by her first husband, John Gray; Sir Anthony Woodville, Lord Rivers, Richard III's rival as protector of Edward, Prince of Wales (later Edward V).
5. *Pomfret*] Pontefract Castle in the West Riding of Yorkshire, where Richard II was murdered in 1399.
7. *My brother's children*] Edward, Prince of Wales, and Richard, Duke of York.

Seem hung within my reach.

RATCLIFFE.   Then take 'em to you
And wear them long and worthily; you are
The last remaining male of princely York
(For Edward's boys, the state esteems not of 'em):   15
And therefore on your sovereignty and rule
The commonweal does her dependence make,
And leans upon your highness' able hand.

CATESBY.

And yet tomorrow does the council meet
To fix a day for Edward's coronation: 20
Who can expound this riddle?

GLOSTER.   That can I.
Those lords are each one my approved, good friends,
Of special trust and nearness to my bosom;
And howsoever busy they may seem,
And diligent to bustle in the state,   25
Their zeal goes on no farther than we lead,
And at our bidding stays.

CATESBY.   Yet there is one,
And he amongst the foremost in his power,
Of whom I wish your highness were assured:
For me—perhaps it is my nature's fault—   30
I own, I doubt of his inclining, much.

GLOSTER.

I guess the man at whom your words would point:
Hastings—

CATESBY.   The same.

GLOSTER.   He bears me great good will.

CATESBY.

'Tis true, to you, as to the Lord Protector
And Gloster's duke, he bows with lowly service: 35
But were he bid to cry, "God save King Richard,"

---

18. highness'] *D2;* highness's *Q,*   31. I own] *Q, Op, Sp; D2 omits* I
Op, Sp.   *(dropped type).*

---

14. *last remaining male*] Edmund, Earl of Rutland, killed at Wakefield
1460; Edward IV, died 1483; George, Duke of Clarence, died 1478.
    15. *esteems not of 'em*] does not value them highly.
    25. *to bustle*] hurry noisily; see Shakespeare's *Richard III,* I.i.152.
    31. *inclining*] willingness to be influenced.

Then tell me in what terms he would reply.
Believe me, I have proved the man and found him.
I know he bears a most religious reverence
To his dead master Edward's royal memory,   40
And whither that may lead him is most plain;
Yet more: one of that stubborn sort he is
Who, if they once grow fond of an opinion,
They call it honor, honesty, and faith,
And sooner part with life than let it go.   45

GLOSTER.
And yet, this tough, impracticable heart
Is governed by a dainty-fingered girl.
Such flaws are found in the most worthy natures;
A laughing, toying, wheedling, whimpering she
Shall make him amble on a gossip's message,   50
And take the distaff with a hand as patient
As e'er did Hercules.

RATCLIFFE.   The fair Alicia,
Of noble birth and exquisite of feature,
Has held him long a vassal to her beauty.

CATESBY.
I fear he fails in his allegiance there;   55
Or my intelligence is false, or else
The dame has been too lavish of her feast,
And fed him till he loathes.

GLOSTER.   No more, he comes.

Enter Lord Hastings.

LORD HASTINGS.
Health and the happiness of many days
Attend upon your grace.

GLOSTER.   My good Lord Chamberlain!   60
We're much beholden to your gentle friendship.

---

38. *proved . . . him*] tested the man and know his convictions.

50. *amble . . . message*] go on a woman's errands; see Shakespeare's *Richard III*, I.i.83.

51. *distaff*] staff on which wool or flax is wound for spinning; see Shakespeare's *King Lear*, IV.ii.17.

52. *Hercules*] son of Zeus and Alcmene. Fifty of his wives conceived in a single night! See Shakespeare's *Much Ado About Nothing*, II.i.261.

13

LORD HASTINGS.

My lord, I come an humble suitor to you.

GLOSTER.

In right good time! Speak out your pleasure freely.

LORD HASTINGS.

I am to move your highness in behalf
Of Shore's unhappy wife.

GLOSTER.   Say you? of Shore?   65

LORD HASTINGS.

Once a bright star that held her place on high:
The first and fairest of our English dames
While royal Edward held the sovereign rule.
Now sunk in grief, and pining with despair,
Her waning form no longer shall incite   70
Envy in woman, or desire in man.
She never sees the sun but through her tears,
And wakes to sigh the livelong night away.

GLOSTER.

Marry! the times are badly changed with her
From Edward's days to these. Then all was jollity,   75
Feasting and mirth, light wantonness and laughter,
Piping and playing, minstrelsy and masquing,
Till life fled from us like an idle dream,
A show of mommery without a meaning.
My brother—rest and pardon to his soul!—   80
Is gone to his account; for this his minion,
The revel-rout is done. —But you were speaking
Concerning her. I have been told that you
Are frequent in your visitation to her.

LORD HASTINGS.

No farther, my good lord, than friendly pity   85
And tender-hearted charity allow.

---

76. Feasting and] D2; Feasting,   account: Sp; account; Op.
and Q, Op, Sp.   81. minion]D2; minion. Q; minion
81. account] Q; account, D2;   Op; minion; Sp.

---

74. *Marry!*] euphemistic respelling of (the Virgin) Mary; exclamation of surprise or indignation.

79. *mommery*] mummery, a pretentious or hypocritical ceremony or show.

81. *minion*] favorite.

GLOSTER.
>Go to! I did not mean to chide you for it.
>For, sooth to say, I hold it noble in you
>To cherish the distressed. —On with your tale.

LORD HASTINGS.
>Thus is it, gracious sir, that certain officers,   90
>Using the warrant of your mighty name,
>With insolence unjust and lawless power
>Have seized upon the lands which late she held
>By grant from her great master Edward's bounty.

GLOSTER.
>Somewhat of this, but slightly, have I heard;   95
>And though some counsellors of forward zeal,
>Some of most ceremonious sanctity
>And bearded wisdom, often have provoked
>The hand of justice to fall heavy on her,
>Yet still in kind compassion of her weakness   100
>And tender memory of Edward's love,
>I have withheld the merciless, stern law
>From doing outrage on her helpless beauty.

LORD HASTINGS.
>Good heav'n, who renders mercy back for mercy,
>With open-handed bounty shall repay you: 105
>This gentle deed shall fairly be set foremost,
>To screen the wild escapes of lawless passion
>And the long train of frailties flesh is heir to.

GLOSTER.
>Thus far, the voice of pity pleaded only;
>Our farther and more full extent of grace   110
>Is given to your request. Let her attend,
>And to ourself deliver up her griefs.
>She shall be heard with patience, and each wrong
>At full redressed. But I have other news
>Which much import us both, for still my fortunes   115
>Go hand in hand with yours; our common foes,

90. is it] *Q, D2;* it is *Op, Sp.*

---

87. *Go to!*] Come now!
115. *import*] concerns.

15

    The queen's relations, our new-fangled gentry,
    Have fall'n their haughty crests.—That for your
        privacy.   *Exeunt.*

[I.ii]   *An apartment in Jane Shore's house.*
           Enter Bellmour *and* Dumont.

BELLMOUR.

    How she has lived, you've heard my tale already;
    The rest, your own attendance in her family,
    Where I have found the means this day to place you,
    And nearer observation best will tell you.
    See! with what sad and sober cheer she comes.   5
            Enter Jane Shore.

    Sure, or I read her visage much amiss,
    Or grief besets her hard. —Save you, fair lady,
    The blessings of the cheerful morn be on you,
    And greet your beauty with its opening sweets.

JANE SHORE.

    My gentle neighbor! your good wishes still   10
    Pursue my hapless fortunes. Ah! good Bellmour!
    How few, like thee, enquire the wretched out,
    And court the offices of soft humanity;
    Like thee, reserve their raiment for the naked,
    Reach out their bread to feed the crying orphan,   15
    Or mix their pitying tears with those that weep!
    Thy praise deserves a better tongue than mine
    To speak and bless thy name. Is this the gentleman
    Whose friendly service you commended to me?

117. new-fangled] *D2;* new fangl'd
Q, Op. ᵒₚ.

---

   117. *new-fangled gentry*] the Woodvilles, citizens newly raised to status
just below the nobility.
   118. *fall'n . . . crests*] have lost their heads on the block. See Shakespeare's *Troilus and Cressida,* II.i.379–380; *Julius Caesar,* IV.ii.26.
[I.ii]
   5. *cheer*] mood.
   6–7. *or . . . Or*] either . . . Or
   12–16.] See Isaiah 58:7: "Is it not to deal thy bread to the hungry, and
that thou bring the poor that are cast out to thy house? . . . ."

BELLMOUR.

    Madam! it is.

JANE SHORE *(aside).* A venerable aspect!   20
    Age sits with decent grace upon his visage,
    And worthily becomes his silver locks;
    He wears the marks of many years well spent,
    Of virtue, truth well tried, and wise experience;
    A friend like this would suit my sorrows well.—   25
    (To Dumont.)   Fortune, I fear me, sir, has meant you ill,
    Who pays your merit with that scanty pittance
    Which my poor hand and humble roof can give.
    But to supply those golden vantages
    Which elsewhere you might find, expect to meet   30
    A just regard and value for your worth,
    The welcome of a friend, and the free partnership
    Of all that little good the world allows me.

DUMONT.

    You overrate me much, and all my answer
    Must be my future truth; let that speak for me   35
    And make up my deserving.

JANE SHORE.   Are you of England?

DUMONT.

    No, gracious lady, Flanders claims my birth;
    At Antwerp has my constant biding been,
    Where sometimes I have known more plenteous days
    Than those which now my failing age affords.   40

JANE SHORE.

    Alas! at Antwerp! *(Weeping.)*   Oh, forgive my tears!
    They fall for my offenses—and must fall
    Long, long ere they shall wash my stains away.
    You knew perhaps—oh grief! oh shame!—my husband.

DUMONT.

    I knew him well—but stay this flood of anguish;   45
    The senseless grave feels not your pious sorrows.
    Three years and more are past since I was bid,
    With many of our common friends, to wait him
    To his last peaceful mansion. I attended,

---

28. roof] *D2, Op, Sp;* proof *Q.*

---

37. *Flanders*] modern Belgium.

    Sprinkled his clay-cold corse with holy drops,   50
    According to our church's reverend rite,
    And saw him laid, in hallowed ground, to rest.

JANE SHORE.

    Oh! that my soul had known no joy but him;
    That I had lived within his guiltless arms,
    And dying slept in innocence beside him!   55
    But now his honest dust abhors the fellowship,
    And scorns to mix with mine.

Enter a Servant.

SERVANT.   The lady Alicia
    Attends your leisure.

JANE SHORE.   Say I wish to see her.   *Exit* Servant.
    Please, gentle sir, one moment to retire.
    I'll wait you on the instant, and inform you   60
    Of each unhappy circumstance in which
    Your friendly aid and counsel much may stead me.

                  Exeunt Bellmour *and* Dumont.

Enter Alicia.

ALICIA.

    Still, fair friend, still shall I find you thus?
    Still shall these sighs heave after one another,
    These trickling drops chase one another still,   65
    As if the posting messengers of grief
    Could overtake the hours fled far away,
    And make old time come back?

JANE SHORE.   No, my Alicia,
    Heaven and its saints be witness to my thoughts,
    There is no hour of all my life o'erpast,   70
    That I could wish should take its turn again.

ALICIA.

    And yet some of those days my friend has known,
    Some of those years might pass for golden ones—
    At least, if womankind can judge of happiness.
    What could we wish, we who delight in empire,   75
    Whose beauty is our sovereign good, and gives us
    Our reasons to rebel and power to reign?

---

73. *Some of those years*] i.e., 1461 to 1483.

What could we more than to behold a monarch,
Lovely, renowned, a conqueror, and young,
Bound in our chains, and sighing at our feet?   80
JANE SHORE.
'Tis true, the royal Edward was a wonder,
The goodly pride of all our English youth;
He was the very joy of all that saw him,
Formed to delight, to love, and to persuade.
Impassive spirits and angelic natures   85
Might have been charmed, like yielding human
    weakness,
Stooped from their heav'n and listened to his talking.
But what had I to do with kings and courts?
My humble lot had cast me far beneath him;
And that he was the first of all mankind,   90
The bravest and most lovely, was my curse.
ALICIA.
Sure, something more than fortune joined your loves;
Nor could his greatness, and his gracious form,
Be elsewhere matched so well, as to the sweetness
And beauty of my friend.
JANE SHORE.   Name him no more: 95
He was the bane and ruin of my peace.
This anguish and these tears, these are the legacies
His fatal love has left me. Thou wilt see me;
Believe me, my Alicia, thou wilt see me,
Ere yet a few short days pass o'er my head,   100
Abandoned to the very utmost wretchedness.
The hand of pow'r has seized almost the whole
Of what was left for needy life's support;
Shortly thou wilt behold me poor, and kneeling
Before thy charitable door for bread.   105
ALICIA.
Joy of my life, my dearest Shore, forbear
To wound my heart with thy forboding sorrows.
Raise thy sad soul to better hopes than these;
Lift up thine eyes and let 'em shine once more,

91. lovely, was] *D2, Sp;* lovely was
Q, Op.
113. Spite] *Q, Op, Sp;* Spyht *D2.*

19

Bright as the morning sun above the mists.   110
Exert thy charms, seek out the stern Protector,
And soothe his savage temper with thy beauty.
Spite of his deadly, unrelenting nature,
He shall be moved to pity and redress thee.

JANE SHORE.

My form, alas! has long forgot to please.   115
The scene of beauty and delight has changed:
No roses bloom upon my fading cheek,
Nor laughing graces wanton in my eyes;
But haggard grief, lean-looking, sallow care,
And pining discontent, a rueful train,   120
Dwell on my brow, all hideous and forlorn.
One only shadow of a hope is left me;
The noble-minded Hastings, of his goodness,
Has kindly underta'en to be my advocate,
And move my humble suit to angry Gloster.   125

ALICIA.

Does Hastings undertake to plead your cause?
But wherefore should he not? Hastings has eyes;
The gentle lord has a right tender heart,
Melting and easy, yielding to impression,
And catching the soft flame from each new beauty. 130
But yours shall charm him long.

JANE SHORE.   Away, you flatterer!
Nor charge his generous meaning with a weakness
Which his great soul and virtue must disdain.
Too much of love thy hapless friend has proved;
Too many giddy, foolish hours are gone,   135
And in fantastic measures danced away:
May the remaining few know only friendship.
So thou, my dearest, truest, best Alicia,
Vouchsafe to lodge me in thy gentle heart
A partner there; I will give up mankind,   140
Forget the transports of increasing passion,
And all the pangs we feel for its decay.

ALICIA.

Live! live and reign forever in my bosom;   *Embracing.*
Safe and unrivalled there possess thy own;
And you, ye brightest of the stars above,   145

Ye saints that once were women here below,
Be witness of the truth, the holy friendship,
Which here to this my other self I vow.
If I not hold her nearer to my soul
Than ev'ry other joy the world can give, 150
Let poverty, deformity and shame,
Distraction and despair seize me on earth;
Let not my faithless ghost have peace hereafter,
Nor taste the bliss of your celestial fellowship.

JANE SHORE.
Yes, thou art true, and only thou art true; 155
Therefore these jewels, once the lavish bounty
Of royal Edward's love, I trust to thee.   *Giving a casket.*
Receive this all that I can call my own,
And let it rest unknown and safe with thee:
That if the state's injustice should oppress me, 160
Strip me of all, and turn me out a wanderer,
My wretchedness may find relief from thee,
And shelter from the storm.

ALICIA.   My all is thine;
One common hazard shall attend us both,
And both be fortunate, or both be wretched. 165
But let thy fearful, doubting heart be still;
The saints and angels have thee in their charge,
And all things shall be well. Think not, the good,
The gentle deeds of mercy thou hast done
Shall die forgotten all; the poor, the pris'ner, 170
The fatherless, the friendless, and the widow,
Who daily own the bounty of thy hand,
Shall cry to heav'n, and pull a blessing on thee;
Ev'n man—the merciless insulter, man—
Man, who rejoices in our sex's weakness, 175
Shall pity thee, and with unwonted goodness,
Forget thy failings and record thy praise.

JANE SHORE
Why should I think that man will do for me

---

169. *The gentle ... mercy*] Jane Shore's reputation for gaining royal
favors, pardons for those under royal censure, and her support of
churches and other philanthropies is mentioned by all historians of her
ruin.

21

What yet he never did for wretches like me?
Mark by what partial justice we are judged;   180
Such is the fate unhappy women find,
And such the curse entailed upon our kind,
That man, the lawless libertine, may rove
Free and unquestioned through the wilds of love;
While woman, sense and nature's easy fool,   185
If poor, weak woman swerve from virtue's rule,
If, strongly charmed, she leave the thorny way,
And in the softer paths of pleasure stray,
Ruin ensues, reproach and endless shame,
And one false step entirely damns her fame.   190
In vain with tears the loss she may deplore,
In vain look back to what she was before;
She sets, like stars that fall, to rise no more.   *Exeunt.*

End of the First Act

---

182. *entailed . . . kind*] inherited from Eve, the first woman.

ACT II

Scene continues.
Enter Alicia *(speaking to* Jane Shore *as entering).*

ALICIA.
    No farther, gentle friend; good angels guard you,
    And spread their gracious wings about your slumbers.—
    The drowsy night grows on the world, and now
    The busy craftsman and the o'er-labored hind
    Forget the travail of the day in sleep.   5
    Care only wakes, and moping pensiveness;
    With meagre, discontented looks they sit,
    And watch the wasting of the midnight taper.
    Such vigils must I keep; so wakes my soul,
    Restless and self-tormented! O false Hastings!   10
    Thou hast destroyed my peace.   *Knocking without.*
                      What noise is that?
    What visitor is this who with bold freedom
    Breaks in upon the peaceful night and rest
    With such a rude approach?

Enter a Servant.

SERVANT.   One from the court,
    Lord Hastings (as I think) demands my lady.   15
ALICIA.
    Hastings! Be still my heart, and try to meet him
    With his own arts—with falsehood. —But he comes.

Enter Lord Hastings.

LORD HASTINGS *(speaks to a* Servant *at entering).*
    Dismiss my train and wait alone without.
    [*Aside.*]   Alicia here! Unfortunate encounter!
    But be it as it may.
ALICIA.   When humbly, thus   20
    The great descend to visit the afflicted;
    When thus unmindful of their rest, they come
    To soothe the sorrows of the midnight mourner;
    Comfort comes with them, like the golden sun,

---

4. *hind*] farm laborer.

Dispels the sullen shades with her sweet influence,   25
And cheers the melancholy house of care.

LORD HASTINGS.

'Tis true, I would not overrate a courtesy,
Nor let the coldness of delay hang on it
To nip and blast its favor like a frost;
But rather chose, at this late hour, to come,   30
That your fair friend may know I have prevailed:
The Lord Protector has received her suit,
And means to show her grace.

ALICIA.   My friend! my lord!

LORD HASTINGS.

Yes, lady, yours: none has a right more ample
To task my power than you.

ALICIA.   I want the words   35
To pay you back a compliment so courtly;
But my heart guesses at the friendly meaning,
And wo' not die your debtor.

LORD HASTINGS.   'Tis well, madam,
But I would see your friend.

ALICIA.   O thou false lord!
I would be mistress of my heaving heart,   40
Stifle this rising rage, and learn from thee
To dress my face in easy, dull indifference.
But 't wo'not be; my wrongs will tear their way,
And rush at once upon thee.

LORD HASTINGS.   Are you wise?
Have you the use of reason? Do you wake?   45
What means this raving, this transporting passion?

ALICIA.

O thou cool traitor, thou insulting tyrant!
Dost thou behold my poor distracted heart,
Thus rent with agonizing love and rage,
And ask me what it means? Art thou not false?   50
Am I not scorned, forsaken, and abandoned,
Left, like a common wretch, to shame and infamy,
Giv'n up to be the sport of villains' tongues,
Of laughing parasites, and lewd buffoons,
And all because my soul has doted on thee   55
With love, with truth, and tenderness unutterable?

24

LORD HASTINGS.

>Are these the proofs of tenderness and love?
>These endless quarrels, discontents, and jealousies,
>These never-ceasing wailings and complainings,
>These furious starts, these whirlwinds of the soul,   60
>Which every other moment rise to madness?

ALICIA.

>What proof, alas! have I not given of love?
>What have I not abandoned to thy arms?
>Have I not set at nought my noble birth,
>A spotless fame and an unblemished race,   65
>The peace of innocence and pride of virtue?
>My prodigality has giv'n thee all;
>And now I have nothing left me to bestow;
>You hate the wretched bankrupt you have made.

LORD HASTINGS.

>Why am I thus pursued from place to place,   70
>Kept in the view, and crossed at every turn?
>In vain I fly, and like a hunted deer
>Scud o'er the lawns and hasten to the covert;
>Ere I can reach my safety, you o'ertake me
>With the swift malice of some keen reproach,   75
>And drive the winged shaft deep in my heart.

ALICIA.

>Hither you fly, and here you seek repose;
>Spite of the poor deceit, your arts are known,
>Your pious, charitable, midnight visits.

LORD HASTINGS.

>If you are wise and prize your peace of mind,   80
>Yet take the friendly counsel of my love;
>Believe me true, nor listen to your jealousy;
>Let not that devil which undoes your sex,
>That cursed curiosity, seduce you
>To hunt for needless secrets which, neglected,   85
>Shall never hurt your quiet, but once known,
>Shall sit upon your heart, pinch it with pain,
>And banish the sweet sleep forever from you.
>Go to!—be yet advised—

68. I have] *Q, Op, Sp;* I've *D2.*   89. Go to!] Go too *Q, D2, Op, Sp.*
83. undoes] *D2;* undo's *Q, Op, Sp.*

ALICIA.   Dost thou in scorn
      Preach patience to my rage? and bid me tamely   90
      Sit like a poor, contented idiot down,
      Nor dare to think thou'st wronged me?—Ruin seize
            thee,
      And swift perdition overtake thy treachery!
      Have I the least remaining cause to doubt?
      Hast thou endeavored once to hide thy falsehood?   95
      To hide it might have spoke some little tenderness,
      And shown thee half unwilling to undo me.
      But thou disdain'st the weakness of humanity;
      Thy words and all thy actions have confessed it.
      Ev'n now thy eyes avow it, now they speak,   100
      And insolently own the glorious villainy.
LORD HASTINGS.
      Well then, I own my heart has broke your chains.
      Patient I bore the painful bondage long:
      At length my generous love disdains your tyranny;
      The bitterness and stings of taunting jealousy,   105
      Vexatious days, and jarring joyless nights,
      Have driv'n him forth to seek some safer shelter,
      Where he may rest his weary wings in peace.
ALICIA.
      You triumph! do! And with gigantic pride
      Defy impending vengeance. Heav'n shall wink;   110
      No more his arm shall roll the dreadful thunder,
      Nor send his light'nings forth. No more his justice
      Shall visit the presuming sons of men,
      But perjury, like thine, shall dwell in safety.
LORD HASTINGS.
      Whate'er my fate decrees for me hereafter,   115
      Be present to me now, my better angel!
      Preserve me from the storm which threatens now,
      And if I have beyond atonement sinned,
      Let any other kind of plague o'ertake me,
      So I escape the fury of that tongue.   120
ALICIA.
      Thy pray'r is heard—I go; but know, proud lord,

92. thou'st] *D2;* thou hast *Q, Op,*
Sp.

Howe'er thou scorn'st the weakness of my sex,
This feeble hand may find the means to reach thee,
Howe'er sublime in pow'r and greatness placed,
With royal favor guarded round and graced;   125
On eagle's wings my rage shall urge her flight,
And hurl thee headlong from thy topmost height;
Then like thy fate, superior will I sit,
And view thee fall'n and groveling at my feet;
See thy last breath with indignation go,   130
And tread thee sinking to the shades below.   *Exit* Alic[ia].

LORD HASTINGS.

How fierce a fiend is passion. With what wildness,
What tyranny untamed, it reigns in woman.
Unhappy sex! whose easy, yielding temper
Gives way to every appetite alike;   135
Each gust of inclination, uncontrolled,
Sweeps through their souls and sets 'em in an uproar;
Each motion of the heart rises to fury,
And love in their weak bosoms is a rage
As terrible as hate and as destructive.   140
So the wind roars o'er the wide fenceless ocean,
And heaves the billows of the boiling deep,
Alike from north, from south, from east, and west;
With equal force the tempest blows by turns
From every corner of the seaman's compass.   145
But soft ye now—for here comes one disclaims
Strife and her wrangling train. Of equal elements
Without one jarring atom, was she formed,
And gentleness and joy make up her being.—

Enter Jane Shore.

Forgive me, fair one, if officious friendship   150
Intrudes on your repose, and comes thus late
To greet you with the tidings of success.
The princely Gloster has vouchsafed you hearing;
Tomorrow he expects you at the court.

126. eagle's] eagles *Q, D2, Op, Sp*.   138. of the] *Q, Sp;* of their *D2, Op.*
129. groveling] *Q, Op, Sp;* grov'-   143. and west] *Q, Op, Sp;* from
ling *D2*.   West *D2.*
132. fiend] *D2, Op;* friend *Q, Sp.*

150. *officious friendship*] oversolicitous friendship.

27

There plead your cause with never-failing beauty;   155
Speak all your griefs and find a full redress.

JANE SHORE *(kneeling).*

Thus humbly let your lowly servant bend;
Thus let me bow my grateful knee to earth,
And bless your noble nature for this goodness.

LORD HASTINGS.

Rise, gentle dame. You wrong my meaning much;   160
Think me not guilty of a thought so vain,
To sell my courtesy for thanks like these.

JANE SHORE.

'Tis true, your bounty is beyond my speaking;
But though my mouth be dumb, my heart shall thank
    you;
And when it melts before the throne of mercy,   165
Mourning and bleeding for my past offenses,
My fervent soul shall breathe one prayer for you,
If prayers of such a wretch are heard on high,
That heav'n will pay you back when you most need
The grace and goodness you have shown to me.   170

LORD HASTINGS.

If there be aught of merit in my service,
Impute it there where most 'tis due, to love;
Be kind, my gentle mistress, to my wishes,
And satisfy my panting heart with beauty.

JANE SHORE.

Alas! my lord—

LORD HASTINGS.   Why bend thy eyes to earth?   175
Wherefore these looks of heaviness and sorrow?
Why breathes that sigh, my love? And wherefore falls
This trickling show'r of tears to stain thy sweetness?

JANE SHORE.

If pity dwells within your noble breast
(As sure it does), oh, speak not to me thus!   180

LORD HASTINGS.

Can I behold thee and not speak of love?
Ev'n now, thus sadly as thou stand'st before me,

---

172. there where most 'tis] *D2, Op,*   178. tears] *D2, Op, Sp;* teats *Q.*
Sp; there, where most is *Q.*

Thus desolate, dejected, and forlorn,
Thy softness steals upon my yielding senses
Till my soul faints and sickens with desire.   185
How canst thou give this motion to my heart,
And bid my tongue be still?

JANE SHORE.   Cast round your eyes
Upon the highborn beauties of the court;
Behold, like opening roses, where they bloom,
Sweet to the sense, unsullied all, and spotless.   190
There choose some worthy partner of your heart,
To fill your arms and bless your virtuous bed,
Nor turn you eyes this way, where sin and misery,
Like loathsome weeds, have overrun the soil,
And the destroyer shame has laid all waste.   195

LORD HASTINGS.
What means this peevish, this fantastic change?
Where is thy wonted pleasantness of face?
Thy wonted graces, and thy dimpled smiles?
Where hast thou lost thy wit and sportive mirth,
That cheerful heart, which used to dance forever,   200
And cast a day of gladness all around thee?

JANE SHORE.
Yes, I will own I merit the reproach,
And for those foolish days of wanton pride
My soul is justly humbled to the dust.
All tongues, like yours, are licensed to upbraid me, 205
Still to repeat my guilt, to urge my infamy,
And treat me like the abject thing I have been.
Yet let the saints be witness to this truth,
That now, though late, I look with horror back,
That I detest my wretched self, and curse   210
My past polluted life. All-judging heav'n,
Who knows my crimes, has seen my sorrow for them.

LORD HASTINGS.
No more of this dull stuff. 'Tis time enough
To whine and mortify thyself with penance
When the decaying sense is palled with pleasure,   215

202. reproach,] *D2;* reproach? *Q,*
Op; reproach: *Sp.*

---

196. *fantastic*] unreal, insane.

29

And weary nature tires in her last stage.
Then weep and tell thy beads, when alt'ring rheums
Have stained the luster of thy starry eyes,
And failing palsies shake thy withered hand.
The present moments claim more generous use;   220
Thy beauty, night, and solitude reproach me
For having talked thus long. Come, let me press thee,

                                    Laying hold on her.

Pant on thy bosom, sink into thy arms
And lose myself in the luxurious fold.

JANE SHORE.

Never! By those chaste lights above, I swear,   225
My soul shall never know pollution more!
Forbear, my lord! Here let me rather die;   *Kneeling.*
Let quick destruction overtake me here,
And end my sorrows and my shame forever.

LORD HASTINGS.

Away with this perverseness; 'tis too much.   *Striving.*   230
Nay, if you strive—'tis monstrous affectation.

JANE SHORE.

Retire! I beg you, leave me—

LORD HASTINGS.   Thus to coy it!—
With one who knows you, too!

JANE SHORE.   For mercy's sake—

LORD HASTINGS.

Ungrateful woman! is it thus you pay
My services?

JANE SHORE.   Abandon me to ruin   235
Rather than urge me—

LORD HASTINGS *(pulling her)*. This way to your chamber;
There if you struggle—

JANE SHORE *(crying out)*.

Help! O gracious heaven!
Help! Save me! Help!

                Enter Dumont; *he interposes.*

227. die;] die *Q, Op, Sp;* die, *D2.*   233. mercy's] mercies *Q, D2, Op, Sp.*

232. *Thus to coy it*] pretend to be modest; see Shakespeare's *Taming of the Shrew,* II.i.245.

DUMONT.   My lord! for honor's sake—

LORD HASTINGS.

Hah! What art thou?—Begone!

DUMONT.   My duty calls me

To my attendance on my mistress here.   240

JANE SHORE.

For pity let me go!

LORD HASTINGS.   Avaunt! base groom;

At distance wait and know thy office better.

DUMONT.

Forgo your hold, my lord! 'tis most unmanly

This violence—

LORD HASTINGS.   Avoid the room this moment,

Or I will tread thy soul out.

DUMONT.   No, my lord;   245

The common ties of manhood call me now,

And bid me thus stand up in the defense

Of an oppressed, unhappy, helpless woman.

LORD HASTINGS.

And dost thou know me? Slave!

DUMONT.   Yes, thou proud lord!

I know thee well, know thee with each advantage   250

Which wealth, or power, or noble birth can give thee.

I know thee, too, for one who stains those honors,

And blots a long illustrious line of ancestry,

By poorly daring thus to wrong a woman.

LORD HASTINGS.

'Tis wondrous well! I see, my saint-like dame,   255

You stand provided of your braves and ruffians

To man your cause, and bluster in your brothel.

DUMONT.

Take back the foul reproach, unmannered railer,

Nor urge my rage too far, lest thou shouldst find

I have as daring spirits in my blood   260

As thou or any of thy race e'er boasted.

238. honor's] *D2, Op;* honors *Q,*   259. lest] *D2;* least *Q, Op, Sp.*
Sp.   259. shouldst] shou'lst *Q, D2;*
239. Begone!] *D2;* begon *Q, Op,*   should'st *Op, Sp.*
Sp.

---

241. *Avaunt! base groom*] Go away, base servant!

And though no gaudy titles graced my birth—
Titles, the servile courtier's lean reward,
Sometimes the pay of virtue, but more oft
The hire which greatness gives to slaves and
    sycophants—   265
Yet heav'n, that made me honest, made me more
Than ever king did when he made a lord.

LORD HASTINGS.

Insolent villain! Henceforth let this teach thee
                          Draws and strikes him.
The distance 'twixt a peasant and a prince.

DUMONT.

Nay then, my lord!   *(Drawing.)*   Learn you by this
    how well   270
An arm resolved can guard its master's life.   *They fight.*

JANE SHORE.

Oh my distracting fears! hold, for sweet heav'n!

    They fight; Dumont *disarms* Lord Hastings.

LORD HASTINGS.

Confusion! baffled by a base-born hind!

DUMONT.

Now, haughty sir, where is our difference now?
Your life is in my hand, and did not honor,   275
The gentleness of blood, and inborn virtue
(Howe'er unworthy I may seem to you)
Plead in my bosom, I should take the forfeit.
But wear your sword again; and know, a lord
Opposed against a man is but a man.   280

LORD HASTINGS.

Curse on my failing hand! Your better fortune
Has giv'n you vantage o'er me; but perhaps
Your triumph may be bought with dear repentance. *Exit.*

JANE SHORE.

Alas! what have you done! Know you the pow'r,
The mightiness that waits upon this lord?   285

DUMONT.

Fear not, my worthiest mistress; 'tis a cause
In which heav'n's guard shall wait you. Oh, pursue,

___

287. *wait*] escort.

Pursue the sacred counsels of your soul
Which urge you on to virtue; let not danger,
Nor the encumb'ring world, make faint your purpose! 290
Assisting angels shall conduct your steps,
Bring you to bliss, and crown your end with peace.

JANE SHORE.

Oh, that my head were laid, my sad eyes closed,
And my cold corse wound in my shroud to rest;
My painful heart will never cease to beat,   295
Will never know a moment's peace till then.

DUMONT.

Would you be happy? Leave this fatal place,
Fly from the court's pernicious neighborhood,
Where innocence is shamed, and blushing modesty
Is made the scorner's jest; where hate, deceit,   300
And deadly ruin wear the mask of beauty,
And draw deluded fools with shows of pleasure.

JANE SHORE.

Where should I fly, thus helpless and forlorn,
Of friends and all the means of life bereft?

DUMONT.

Bellmour, whose friendly care still wakes to serve you, 305
Has found you out a little peaceful refuge.
Far from the court and the tumultuous city,
Within an ancient forest's ample verge,
There stands a lonely but a healthful dwelling,
Built for convenience and the use of life.   310
Around it fallows, meads, and pastures fair,
A little garden, and a limpid brook,
By nature's own contrivance, seem disposed;
No neighbors but a few poor simple clowns,
Honest and true, with a well-meaning priest.   315
No faction, or domestic fury's rage,
Did e'er disturb the quiet of that place

296. moment's] *D2;* moments *Q,*   307. tumultuous] *D2;* tumultous
Op, Sp.   *Q, Op, Sp.*
298. court's] *D2;* courts *Q, Op, Sp.*

---

305. *wakes*] keeps watch.
311. *fallows, meads*] plowed but unseeded lands, meadows.
314. *clowns*] rustics.

33

When the contending nobles shook the land
With York and Lancaster's disputed sway.
Your virtue, there, may find a safe retreat   320
From the insulting pow'rs of wicked greatness.

JANE SHORE.

Can there be so much happiness in store!
A cell like that is all my hopes aspire to.
Haste then, and thither let us wing our flight,
Ere the clouds gather and the wintry sky   325
Descends in storms to intercept our passage.

DUMONT.

Will you then go? You glad my very soul!
Banish your fears, cast all your cares on me;
Plenty and ease, and peace of mind shall wait you,
And make your latter days of life most happy.   330
O lady!—but I must not, cannot tell you
How anxious I have been for all your dangers,
And how my heart rejoices at your safety.
So when the spring renews the flow'ry field,
And warns the pregnant nightingale to build,   335
She seeks the safest shelter of the wood,
Where she may trust her little tuneful brood,
Where no rude swains her shady cell may know,
No serpents climb, nor blasting winds may blow;
Fond of the chosen place, she views it o'er,   340
Sits there and wanders through the grove no more.
Warbling she charms it each returning night,
And loves it with a mother's dear delight.   *Exeunt.*

End of the Second Act

324. Haste] *Op;* hast *Q, D2, Sp.*   343. mother's] *D2;* mothers *Q, Op,*
337. brood,] *Q, Op, Sp;* brood: *D2.*   *Sp.*

319. *York . . . sway*] the Wars of the Roses, 1453–85.

ACT III

Scene, *the Court.*
Enter Alicia *with a paper.*

ALICIA.

This paper to the great Protector's hand
With care and secrecy must be conveyed;
His bold ambition now avows its aim,
To pluck the crown from Edward's infant brow
And fix it on his own. I know he holds   5
My faithless Hastings adverse to his hopes
And much devoted to the orphan king;
On that I build. This paper meets his doubts,
And marks my hated rival as the cause
Of Hastings' zeal for his dead master's sons.   10
O jealousy! Thou bane of pleasing friendship,
Thou worst invader of our tender bosoms;
How does thy rancor poison all our softness,
And turn our gentle natures into bitterness!—
See where she comes! Once my heart's dearest blessing,   15
Now my changed eyes are blasted with her beauty,
Loathe that known face, and sicken to behold her.

Enter Jane Shore.

JANE SHORE.

Now whither shall I fly to find relief?
What charitable hand will aid me now?
Will stay my failing steps, support my ruins,   20
And heal my wounded mind with balmy comfort?
O my Alicia!
ALICIA.   What new grief is this?
What unforseen misfortune has surprised thee
That racks thy tender heart thus?
JANE SHORE.   Oh! Dumont!
ALICIA.
Say! What of him?
JANE SHORE.   That friendly, honest man,   25

_____

11. *bane*] poison.
20. *ruins*] aging body.

35

Whom Bellmour brought of late to my assistance;
On whose kind cares, whose diligence and faith
My surest trust was built, this very morn
Was seized on by the cruel hand of pow'r,
Forced from my house, and borne away to prison.   30

ALICIA.

To prison, said you! Can you guess the cause?

JANE SHORE.

Too well, I fear. His bold defense of me
Has drawn the vengeance of Lord Hastings on him.

ALICIA.

Lord Hastings! ha!

JANE SHORE.   Some fitter time must tell thee
The tale of my hard hap. Upon the present   35
Hang all my poor, my last remaining hopes.
Within this paper is my suit contained;
Here, as the princely Gloster passes forth,
I wait to give it on my humble knees,
And move him for redress.

She gives the paper to Alicia, *who opens and seems to read it.*

ALICIA *(aside).*   Now for a wile   40
To sting my thoughtless rival to the heart,
To blast her fatal beauties, and divide her
Forever from my perjured Hastings' eyes.
The wanderer may then look back to me,
And turn to his forsaken home again.   45

Pulling out the other paper.

Their fashions are the same; it cannot fail.

JANE SHORE.

But see, the great Protector comes this way,
Attended by a train of waiting courtiers.
Give me the paper, friend.

ALICIA *(aside).*   For love and vengeance!

She gives her the other paper.

Enter the Duke of Gloster, *Sir Richard Ratcliffe, Catesby,* Courtiers, *and other Attendants.*

---

35. *hard hap*] hard luck.
40. *wile*] trick.

JANE SHORE *(kneeling).*

    O noble Gloster, turn thy gracious eye,   50
    Incline thy pitying ear to my complaint!
    A poor, undone, forsaken, helpless woman
    Intreats a little bread for charity,
    To feed her wants and save her life from perishing.

GLOSTER *(receiving the paper, and raising her).*

    Arise, fair dame, and dry your watery eyes.   55
    Beshrew me, but 'twere pity of his heart
    That could refuse a boon to such a suitress.
    Y'have got a noble friend to be your advocate;
    A worthy and right gentle lord he is,
    And to his trust most true. This present now   60
    Some matters of the state detain our leisure;
    Those once dispatched, we'll call for you anon
    And give your griefs redress. Go to! be comforted.

JANE SHORE.

    Good heav'ns repay your highness for this pity,
    And show'r down blessings on your princely head.   65
    Come, my Alicia, reach thy friendly arm,
    And help me to support this feeble frame
    That nodding totters with oppressive woe,
    And sinks beneath its load.

                   Exeunt J[ane] Shore *and* Alicia.

GLOSTER.   Now, by my hollidame!

    Heavy of heart she seems, and sore afflicted.   70
    But thus it is when rude calamity
    Lays its strong gripe upon these mincing minions;
    The dainty gee-gaw forms dissolve at once,
    And shiver at the shock. What says her paper?

                         Seeming to read.

    Ha! What is this? Come nearer, Ratcliffe! Catesby!   75
    Mark the contents, and then divine the meaning. *He reads.*

---

55. watery] *Q;* wat'ry *D2;* watry *Op,*   *Q, D2, Op.*
Sp.   63. Go to!] Go too! *Q, D2, Op, Sp.*
60. present now] *Sp;* present, now,   69. its] *D2, Op;* it's *Q, Sp.*

---

  56. *Beshrew me*] Curse me.
  69. *by my hollidame!*] by all that's sacred!
  72. *mincing minions*] dainty favorites.
  73. *gee-gaw forms*] bauble shapes.

"Wonder not, princely Gloster, at the notice
This paper brings you from a friend unknown.
Lord Hastings is inclined to call you master,
And kneel to Richard, as to England's king;   80
But Shore's bewitching wife misleads his heart,
And draws his service to King Edward's sons.
Drive her away, you break the charm that holds him,
And he, and all his powers, attend on you."

RATCLIFFE.
    'Tis wonderful.

CATESBY.   The means by which it came,   85
    Yet stranger too!

GLOSTER.   You saw it giv'n but now.

RATCLIFFE.
    She could not know the purport.

GLOSTER.   No, 'tis plain—
    She knows it not; it levels at her life;
    Should she presume to prate of such high matters,
    The meddling harlot! dear she should abide it.   90

CATESBY.
    What hand so'er it comes from, be assured,
    It means your highness well—

GLOSTER.   Upon the instant
    Lord Hastings will be here. This morn I mean
    To prove him to the quick; then if he flinch
    No more but this, away with him at once;   95
    He must be mine or nothing. —But he comes!
    Draw nearer this way and observe me well.   *They whisper.*

Enter Lord Hastings.

LORD HASTINGS [*aside*].
    This foolish woman hangs about my heart,
    Lingers and wanders in my fancy still;
    This coyness is put on, 'tis art and cunning,   100
    And worn to urge desire. I must possess her.
    The groom who lift his saucy hand against me
    Ere this is humbled and repents his daring.
    Perhaps ev'n she may profit by th'example,
    And teach her beauty not to scorn my pow'r.   105

38

GLOSTER.

    This do, and wait me ere the council sits.

                  Exeunt Rat[cliffe] *and* Catesby.

    My lord, y'are well encountered; here has been
    A fair petitioner this morning with us.
    Believe me, she has won me much to pity her.
    Alas! her gentle nature was not made   110
    To buffet with adversity. I told her
    How worthily her cause you had befriended,
    How much for your good sake we meant to do,
    That you had spoke and all things should be well.

LORD HASTINGS.

    Your highness binds me ever to your service.   115

GLOSTER.

    You know your friendship is most potent with us,
    And shares our power. But of this enough,
    For we have other matters for your ear.
    The state is out of tune; distracting fears
    And jealous doubts jar in our public councils: 120
    Amidst the wealthy cit murmurs rise,
    Lewd railings and reproach on those that rule,
    With open scorn of government; hence credit
    And public trust 'twixt man and man are broke.
    The golden streams of commerce are withheld,   125
    Which fed the wants of needy hinds and artisans,
    Who therefore curse the great and threat rebellion.

LORD HASTINGS.

    The resty knaves are overrun with ease,
    As plenty ever is the nurse of faction.
    If in good days, like these, the headstrong herd   130
    Grow madly wanton and repine, it is
    Because the reins of pow'r are held too slack,
    And reverend authority of late
    Has worn a face of mercy more than justice.

GLOSTER.

    Beshrew my heart! but you have well divined   135
    The source of these disorders. Who can wonder

---

122. *cit*] short for citizen(s).
126. *hinds and artisans*] farm laborers and craftsmen.
128. *resty*] restive; obstinate in standing still.

If riot and misrule o'erturn the realm
When the crown sits upon a baby brow?
Plainly to speak, hence comes the general cry   140
And sum of all complaint: "'Twill ne'er be well
With England" (thus they talk) "while children govern."

LORD HASTINGS.

'Tis true the king is young; but what of that?
We feel no want of Edward's riper years
While Gloster's valor and most princely wisdom
So well supply our infant sovereign's place—   145
His youth's support, and guardian of his throne.

GLOSTER.

The council (much I'm bound to thank 'em for it)
Have placed a pageant scepter in my hand,
Barren of pow'r, and subject to control,
Scorned by my foes, and useless to my friends.   150
O worthy lord! were mine the rule indeed,
I think I should not suffer rank offense
At large to lord it in the commonweal;
Nor would the realm be rent by discord thus,
Thus fear and doubt betwixt disputed titles.   155

LORD HASTINGS.

Of this I am to learn, as not supposing
A doubt like this—

GLOSTER.   Ay, marry, but there is—
And that of much concern. Have you not heard
How, on a late occasion, Doctor Shaw
Has moved the people much about the lawfulness   160
Of Edward's issue? by right grave authority
Of learning and religion plainly proving
A bastard scion never should be grafted
Upon a royal stock; from thence, at full
Discoursing on my brother's former contract   165

---

146. youth's] *D2;* youths *Q, Op, Sp.*   151. indeed,] *D2, Sp;* indeed. *Q,*
147. for it] *Q, Op;* for't *D2, Sp.*   *Op.*
                                             163. scion] *D2, Sp;* scien *Q, Op.*

---

159. *Doctor Shaw*] The Reverend Doctor Ralph Shaw, brother of London's Lord Mayor Edmund Shaw. Doctor Shaw's sermon at Paul's Cross,
"Spurie vitulamina non agent radices altas" ("Bastard slips do not take deep
roots"), proclaimed the illegitimacy of the sons of Edward IV.

To Lady Elizabeth Lucy, long before
His jolly match with that same buxom widow,
The queen he left behind him—
LORD HASTINGS.   Ill befall
    Such meddling priests, who kindle up confusion,
    And vex the quiet world with their vain scruples!   170
    By heav'n, 'tis done in perfect spite to peace
    As if they feared their trade were at an end
    If laymen should agree. Did not the king,
    Our royal master Edward, in concurrence
    With his estates assembled, well determine   175
    What course the sovereign rule should take hencefor-
        ward?
    When shall the deadly hate of factions cease,
    When shall out long divided land have rest,
    If every peevish, moody malcontent
    Shall set the senseless rabble in an uproar,   180
    Fright them with dangers, and perplex their brains
    Each day with some fantastic, giddy change?
GLOSTER.
    What if the same estates, the Lords and Commons,
    Should alter—
LORD HASTINGS.   What?
GLOSTER.   The order of succession?
LORD HASTINGS.
    Curse on the innovating hand attempts it!   185
    Remember him, the villain, righteous heaven,
    In thy great day of vengeance! Blast the traitor
    And his pernicious counsels; who for wealth,
    For pow'r, the pride of greatness or revenge,
    Would plunge his native land in civil wars.   190

---

168. Ill befall] *Op;* I'll befall *Q, Sp;*   183–184.] *Sp; Q, D2, Op:* "*Glos.*
Ill befal *D2.*   What if some patriot for the public
172–173. As . . . agree] *Sp; Q, D2,*   good/ Should vary your scheme,
Op omit.   new mold the state?"

---

   166. *Lady Elizabeth Lucy*] a mistress of Edward IV, by whom he had
two children. The marriage contract was insisted upon by Archbishop
John Morton, but was denied by the lady herself and by the historians.
   169. *meddling priests*] Doctor Ralph Shaw and the provincial of the
Augustinain Friars, Friar Penker.

GLOSTER.

    You go too far, my lord.

LORD HASTINGS.   Your highness' pardon—

    Have we so soon forgot those days of ruin,

    When York and Lancaster drew forth the battles;

    When, like a matron butchered by her sons,

    And cast beside some common way a spectacle   195

    Of horror and affright to passers-by,

    Our groaning country bled at every vein;

    When murders, rapes, and massacres prevailed;

    When churches, palaces, and cities blazed;

    When insolence and barbarism triumphed,   200

    And swept away distinction? Peasants trod

    Upon the necks of nobles. Low were laid

    The reverend crosier and the holy miter,

    And desolation covered all the land.

    Who can remember this, and not, like me,   205

    Here vow to sheath a dagger in his heart

    Whose damned ambition would renew those horrors,

    And set, once more, that scene of blood before us?

GLOSTER.

    How now! So hot!

LORD HASTINGS.   So brave, and so resolved.

GLOSTER.

    Is then our friendship of so little moment   210

    That you could arm your hand against my life?

LORD HASTINGS.

    I hope your highness does not think I meant it;

    No, heav'n forfend that e'er your princely person

    Should come within the scope of my resentment.

GLOSTER.

    O noble Hastings! nay, I must embrace you!   215

                       Embraces him.

    By holy Paul! y'are a right honest man;

    The time is full of danger and distrust,

191. highness'] *D2;* highness's *Q,*
Op, Sp.

---

    203. *crosier . . . holy miter*] the bishop's staff and headdress.
    213. *forefend*] forbid.
    216. *holy Paul*] St. Paul the Apostle.

And warns us to be wary. Hold me not
Too apt for jealousy and light surmise
If, when I meant to lodge you next my heart,   220
I put your truth to trial. Keep your loyalty,
And live your king and country's best support:
For me, I ask no more than honor gives—
To think me yours, and rank me with your friends.

LORD HASTINGS.

Accept what thanks a grateful heart should pay.   225
O princely Gloster! judge me not ungentle,
Of manners rude, and insolent of speech
If, when the public safety is in question,
My zeal flows warm and eager from my tongue.

GLOSTER.

Enough of this: to deal in wordy compliment   230
Is much against the plainness of my nature.
I judge you by myself, a clear true spirit,
And as such once more join you to my bosom.
Farewell, and be my friend.   [*Embraces him.*]
                                              Exit Gloster.

LORD HASTINGS.   I am not read,
Not skilled and practiced in the arts of greatness,   235
To kindle thus, and give a scope to passion.
The duke is surely noble; but he touched me
Ev'n on the tend'rest point, the master-string
That makes most harmony or discord to me.
I own the glorious subject fires my breast,   240
And my soul's darling passion stands confessed.
Beyond or love's or friendship's sacred band,
Beyond myself I prize my native land.
On this foundation would I build my fame,
And emulate the Greek and Roman name;   245
Think England's peace bought cheaply with my blood,
And die with pleasure for my country's good.   *Exit.*

End of the Third Act

---

226. *ungentle*] not of good birth.
234. *read*] learned.
245. *the Greek and Roman name*] Greek and Roman reputation for the
highest patriotism.

43

ACT IV

Scene continues.
Enter Duke of Gloster, Ratcliffe, *and* Catesby.

GLOSTER.

    This was the sum of all, that he would brook
    No alteration in the present state.
    Marry! at last, the testy gentleman
    Was almost moved to bid us bold defiance;
    But there I dropped the argument, and changing   5
    The first design and purpose of my speech,
    I praised his good affection to young Edward,
    And left him to believe my thoughts like his.
    Proceed we then to this fore-mentioned matter
    As nothing bound or trusting to his friendship.   10

RATCLIFFE.

    Ill does it thus befall. I could have wished
    This lord had stood with us. His friends are wealthy,
    Thereto, his own possessions large and mighty;
    The vassals and dependents on his power
    Firm in adherence, ready, bold, and many.   15
    His name has been of 'vantage to your highness,
    And stood our present purpose much in stead.

GLOSTER.

    This wayward and perverse declining from us
    Has warranted at full the friendly notice
    Which we this morn received. I hold it certain,   20
    This puling, whining harlot rules his reason,
    And prompts his zeal for Edward's bastard brood.

CATESBY.

    If she have such dominion o'er his heart,
    And turn it at her will, you rule her fate
    And should, by inference and apt deduction,   25
    Be arbiter of his. Is not her bread,
    The very means immediate to her being,

1–2. would brook . . . state.] *D2;*   brook . . . state: *Op, Sp.*
wou'd brook; . . . state, *Q;* wou'd   6. purpose] *Q, Op, Sp;* porport *D2.*

---

    3. *testy*] irritably impatient.
    21. *puling*] whimpering.

The bounty of your hand? Why does she live
If not to yield obedience to your pleasure,
To speak, to act, to think as you command?   30
RATCLIFFE.
　　Let her instruct her tongue to bear your message,
　　Teach every grace to smile in your behalf
　　And her deluding eyes to gloat for you;
　　His ductile reason will be wound about,
　　Be led and turned again, say and unsay,   35
　　Receive the yoke, and yield exact obedience.
GLOSTER.
　　Your counsel likes me well; it shall be followed.
　　She waits without, attending on her suit;
　　Go, call her in, and leave us here alone.

　　　　　　　　　　　　　　Exeunt Ratcliffe *and* Catesby.

　　How poor a thing is he, how worthy scorn,   40
　　Who leaves the guidance of imperial manhood
　　To such a paltry piece of stuff as this is—
　　A moppet made of prettiness and pride,
　　That oft'ner does her giddy fancies change
　　Than glittering dewdrops in the sun do colors.   45
　　Now shame upon it! Was our reason given
　　For such a use—to be thus puffed about
　　Like a dry leaf, an idle straw, a feather,
　　The sport of every whiffling blast that blows?
　　Beshrew my heart, but it is wond'rous strange;   50
　　Sure, there is something more than witchcraft in them
　　That masters ev'n the wisest of us all.—

　　　　　　　　　　Enter Jane Shore.

　　Oh! you are come most fitly. We have pondered
　　On this your grievance: and though some there are—
　　Nay, and those great ones too—who would enforce   55
　　The rigor of our power to afflict you
　　And bear a heavy hand, yet fear not you.
　　We've ta'en you to our favor; our protection
　　Shall stand between, and shield you from mishap.
JANE SHORE.
　　The blessings of a heart with anguish broken   60
　　And rescued from despair attend your highness!
　　Alas! my gracious lord! What have I done

To kindle such relentless wrath against me?
If in the days of all my past offenses,
When most my heart was lifted with delight,   65
If I withheld my morsel from the hungry,
Forgot the widows' want, and orphans' cry;
If I have known a good I have not shared,
Nor called the poor to take his portion with me,
Let my worst enemies stand forth and now   70
Deny the succor which I gave not then.

GLOSTER.

Marry, there are, though I believe them not,
Who say you meddle in affairs of state;
That you presume to prattle, like a busybody,
Give your advice, and teach the lords o'th' court   75
What fits the order of the commonweal.

JANE SHORE.

Oh, that the busy world at least in this
Would take example from a wretch like me!
None then would waste their hours in foreign
    thoughts,
Forget themselves and what concerns their peace,   80
To tread the mazes of fantastic falsehood,
To haunt her idle sounds and flying tales
Through all the giddy, noisy courts of rumor.
Malicious slander never would have leisure
To search with prying eyes for faults abroad,   85
If all, like me, considered their own hearts,
And wept the sorrows which they found at home.

GLOSTER.

Go to! I know your power, and though I trust not
To every breath of fame, I'm not to learn
That Hastings is professed your loving vassal.   90
But fair befall your beauty; use it wisely,
And it may stand your fortunes much in stead,
Give back your forfeit land with large increase,
And place you high in safety and in honor.

64–65. *Q, D2, Op; Sp omits.*   67. orphans'] orphans *Q, D2, Sp;*
67. widows'] widows *Q, D2, Sp;*   orphan's *Op.*
widow's *Op.*

66–69. *If I . . . with me*] See note to I.ii.12–16.
89. *I'm not to learn*] I already know.

Nay, I could point a way, the which pursuing,   95
You shall not only bring yourself advantage,
But give the realm much worthy cause to thank you.

JANE SHORE.

Oh! where or how? Can my unworthy hand
Become an instrument of good to any?
Instruct your lowly slave, and let me fly   100
To yield obedience to your dread command.

GLOSTER.

Why, that's well said. Thus then— Observe me well.
The state, for many high and potent reasons,
Deeming my brother Edward's sons unfit
For the imperial weight of England's crown—   105

JANE SHORE (aside).

Alas! for pity.

GLOSTER.   Therefore have resolved
To set aside their unavailing infancy,
And vest the sovereign rule in abler hands.
This, though of great importance to the public,
Hastings, for very peevishness and spleen,   110
Does stubbornly oppose.

JANE SHORE.   Does he? Does Hastings?

GLOSTER.

Ay, Hastings.

JANE SHORE.

Reward him for the noble deed, just heavens!
For this one action guard him and distinguish him
With signal mercies, and with great deliverance.   115
Save him from wrong, adversity, and shame;
Let never-failing honors flourish round him,
And consecrate his name even to time's end;
Let him know nothing else but good on earth,
And everlasting blessedness hereafter.   120

GLOSTER.

How now!

JANE SHORE.

The poor, forsaken, royal little ones!
Shall they be left a prey to savage power?
Can they lift up their harmless hands in vain,
Or cry to heav'n for help and not be heard?   125

Impossible! O gallant, generous Hastings,
Go on, pursue! Assert the sacred cause;
Stand forth, thou proxy of all-ruling Providence,
And save the friendless infants from oppression.
Saints shall assist thee with prevailing prayers,   130
And warring angels combat on thy side.

GLOSTER.

You're passing rich in this same heav'nly speech,
And spend it at your pleasure. Nay, but mark me!
My favor is not bought with words like these.
Go to! You'll teach your tongue another tale.   135

JANE SHORE.

No, though the royal Edward has undone me,
He was my king, my gracious master still.
He loved me too; though 'twas a guilty flame
And fated to my peace, yet still he loved me:
With fondness, and with tenderness he doted,   140
Dwelt in my eyes, and lived but in my smiles.
And can I—oh, my heart abhors the thought—
Stand by and see his children robbed of right?

GLOSTER.

Dare not, ev'n for thy soul, to thwart me further;
None of your arts, your feigning, and your foolery, 145
Your dainty, squeamish coying it, to me!
Go—to your lord, your paramour, begone!
Lisp in his ear, hang wanton on his neck,
And play your monkey gambols over to him.
You know my purpose; look that you pursue it,   150
And make him yield obedience to my will.
Do it—or woe upon thy harlot's head!

JANE SHORE.

Oh, that my tongue had ev'ry grace of speech,
Great and commanding as the breath of kings,
Sweet as the poet's numbers, and prevailing   155

130. Saints] *D2, Op, Sp;* The saints   132. heav'nly] *D2;* heavenly *Q, Op,*
Q.   *Sp.*
                                                              135.   Go to!] *D2;* Go too, *Q, Op, Sp.*

139. *fated*] destined to destroy.
146. *coying it*] bashfulness.
149. *monkey gambols*] lecherous sports.

As soft persuasion to a lovesick maid;
That I had art and eloquence divine
To pay my duty to my master's ashes,
And plead till death the cause of injured innocence!

GLOSTER.

Ha! dost thou brave me, minion? dost thou know   160
How vile, how very a wretch, my pow'r can make thee?
That I can let loose fear, distress, and famine,
To hunt thy heels like hell-hounds through the world?
That I can place thee in such abject state
As help shall never find thee; where repining   165
Thou shalt sit down and gnaw the earth for anguish,
Groan to the pitiless winds without return,
Howl like the midnight wolf amidst the desert,
And curse thy life in bitterness of misery?

JANE SHORE.

Let me be branded for the public scorn,   170
Turned forth and driven to wander like a vagabond;
Be friendless and forsaken, seek my bread
Upon the barren, wild, and desolate waste,
Feed on my sighs, and drink my falling tears,
Ere I consent to teach my lips injustice,   175
Or wrong the orphan who has none to save him.

GLOSTER.

'Tis well—we'll try the temper of your heart.
What ho! Who waits without?

          Enter Ratcliffe, Catesby, *and Attendants.*

RATCLIFFE.   Your highness' pleasure.

GLOSTER.

Go, some of you, and turn this strumpet forth!
Spurn her into the street; there let her perish   180
And rot upon a dunghill. Through the city
See it proclaimed that none, on pain of death,
Presume to give her comfort, food, or harbor.
Who ministers the smallest comfort, dies.

178. highness']*D2, Sp;* highness *Q,*
Op.

177. *temper*] hardness.

Her house, her costly furniture and wealth,   185
The purchase of her loose, luxurious life,
We seize on, for the profit of the state.—
Away! Begone!

JANE SHORE.   O thou most righteous judge,
Humbly, behold, I bow myself to thee,
And own the justice in this hard decree: 190
No longer then my ripe offenses spare,
But what I merit, let me learn to bear.
Yet since 'tis all my wretchedness can give,
For my past crimes my forfeit life receive;
No pity for my sufferings here I crave,   195
And only hope forgiveness in the grave.

            Exit J[ane] Shore, *guarded by* Catesby *and others.*

GLOSTER (*to* Ratcliff[e]).
So much for this. Your project's at an end:
This idle toy, this hilding, scorns my power,
And sets us all at nought. See that a guard
Be ready at my call—

RATCLIFFE.   The council waits   200
Upon your highness' leisure.

GLOSTER.   Bid 'em enter.

Enter the Duke of Buckingham, Earl of Derby, *Bishop of Ely,* Lord
Hastings, *and others, as to the council. The* Duke of Gloster *takes
his place at the upper end; then the rest sit.*

EARL OF DERBY.
In happy times are we assembled here,
To point the day and fix the solemn pomp
For placing England's crown with all due rites
Upon our sovereign Edward's youthful brow.   205

201. highness']*D2, Sp;* highness *Q,*
Op.

---

185. *Her house . . . wealth*] estimated by Sir Thomas More and others
at somewhere between two and three thousand marks (silver coins worth
13*s.* 4*d.*), or between £ 1334 and £ 1984.

197. *project's at an end*] Ratcliffe's sounding-out of Hastings.

198. *hilding*] Doctor Johnson defines this as "a mean woman."

199–200. *See . . . call*] Gloster anticipates the exposure of Lord Hastings.

LORD HASTINGS.

 Some busy, meddling knaves 'tis said there are,
 As such will still be prating, who presume
 To carp and cavil at his royal right.
 Therefore I hold it fitting, with the soonest
 T'appoint the order of the coronation; 210
 So to approve our duty to the king,
 And stay the babbling of such vain gainsayers.

GLOSTER.

 My lords! A set of worthy men you are,
 Prudent and just, and careful for the state.
 Therefore, to your most grave determination, 215
 I yield myself in all things, and demand
 What punishment your wisdom shall think meet
 T'inflict upon those damnable contrivers
 Who shall with potions, charms, and witching drugs
 Practice against our person and our life. 220

LORD HASTINGS.

 So much I hold the king your highness' debtor,
 So precious are you to the commonweal,
 That I presume, not only for myself,
 But in behalf of these my noble brothers,
 To say, whoe'er they be, they merit death. 225

GLOSTER.

 Then judge yourselves; convince your eyes of truth.

         Pulling up his sleeve.

 Behold my arm thus blasted, dry and withered,
 Shrunk like a foul abortion, and decayed,
 Like some untimely product of the seasons,
 Robbed of its properties of strength and office. 230
 This is the sorcery of Edward's wife,
 Who in conjunction with that harlot Shore
 And other like confederate midnight hags,
 By force of potent spells, of bloody characters,

221. highness'] *D2, Sp;* highness's 233. hags] haggs *Q, D2, Op, Sp.*
Q, Op.

---

 209. *with the soonest*] as soon as possible.
 230. *office*] service.
 233. *midnight hags*] witches.
 234. *characters*] letters of the alphabet.

And conjurations horrible to hear,   235
Call fiends and specters from the yawning deep,
And set the ministers of hell at work
To torture and despoil me of my life.

LORD HASTINGS.

If they have done this deed—

GLOSTER.   If they have done it!
Talk'st thou to me of ifs, audacious traitor?   240
Thou art that strumpet witch's chief abettor,
The patron and complotter of her mischiefs,
And joined in this contrivance for my death.
Nay, start not, lords. —What ho! a guard there, sirs!

Enter Guard.

Lord Hastings, I arrest thee of high treason!—   245
Seize him, and bear him instantly away;
He sha'not live an hour. By holy Paul!
I will not dine before his head be brought me!
Ratcliffe, stay you and see that it be done.
The rest that love me, rise and follow me.   250

Exeunt Gloster, *and Lords following. Manent* Lord Hastings, Ratcliffe, *and Guard.*

LORD HASTINGS.

What! and no more but this—how! to the scaffold?
O gentle Ratcliffe! tell me, do I hold thee?
Or if I dream, what shall I do to wake,
To break, to struggle through this dread confusion?
For surely death itself is not so painful   255
As is this sudden horror and surprise.

RATCLIFFE.

You heard; the duke's commands to me were absolute.
Therefore, my lord, address you to your shrift
With all good speed you may. Summon your courage,
And be yourself; for you must die this instant.   260

---

241. *strumpet witch's*] Jane Shore's.
243. *complotter*] conspirator.
252. *hold*] hinder.
258. *shrift*] confession and absolution; see Shakespeare's *Richard III*,
III.iv.97.

LORD HASTINGS.
>Yes, Ratcliffe, I will take thy friendly counsel,
>And die as a man should. 'Tis somewhat hard
>To call my scattered spirits home at once;
>But since what must be, must be—let necessity
>Supply the place of time and preparation,   265
>And arm me for the blow. 'Tis but to die;
>'Tis but to venture on that common hazard
>Which many a time in battle I have run;
>'Tis but to do what, at that very moment,
>In many nations of the peopled earth,   270
>A thousand and a thousand shall do with me;
>'Tis but to close my eyes and shut out daylight,
>To view no more the wicked ways of men,
>No longer to behold the tyrant Gloster,
>And be a weeping witness of the woes,   275
>The desolation, slaughter, and calamities,
>Which he shall bring on this unhappy land.

Enter Alicia.

ALICIA.
>Stand off! and let me pass— I will, I must
>Catch him once more in these despairing arms,
>And hold him to my heart. —O Hastings, Hastings! 280
LORD HASTINGS.
>Alas! Why com'st thou at this dreadful moment,
>To fill me with new terrors, new distractions,
>To turn me wild with thy distempered rage,
>And shock the peace of my departing soul?
>Away! I prithee, leave me!
ALICIA.   Stop a minute—   285
>Till my full griefs find passage. —Oh, the tyrant!
>Perdition fall on Gloster's head and mine.
LORD HASTINGS.
>What means thy frantic grief?
ALICIA.   I cannot speak—
>But I have murdered thee. —Oh, I would tell thee—!

289. would] *Q, Op, Sp;* could *D2.*

---

286. *passage*] expression.

53

LORD HASTINGS.

    Speak, and give ease to thy conflicting passions.   290
    Be quick, nor keep me longer in suspense:
    Time presses, and a thousand crowding thoughts
    Break in at once. This way and that they snatch,
    They tear my hurried soul. All claim attention,
    And yet not one is heard. Oh, speak and leave me,   295
    For I have business would employ an age,
    And but a minute's time to get it done in.

ALICIA.

    That, that's my grief—'tis I that urge thee on,
    Thus hunt thee to the toil, sweep thee from earth,
    And drive thee down this precipice of fate.   300

LORD HASTINGS.

    Thy reason is grown wild. Could thy weak hand
    Bring on this mighty ruin? If it could
    What have I done so grievous to thy soul,
    So deadly, so beyond the reach of pardon,
    That nothing but my life can make atonement?   305

ALICIA.

    Thy cruel scorn had stung me to the heart,
    And set my burning bosom all in flames.
    Raving and mad I flew to my revenge,
    And writ I know not what—told the Protector,
    That Shore's detested wife by wiles had won thee   310
    To plot against his greatness. He believed it
    (Oh, dire event of my pernicious counsel!),
    And while I meant destruction on her head,
    H'as turned it all on thine.

LORD HASTINGS.   Accursed jealousy!

    O merciless, wild, and unforgiving fiend!   315
    Blindfold it runs to undistinguished mischief,
    And murders all it meets. Curst be its rage,
    For there is none so deadly; doubly curst
    Be all those easy fools who give it harbor,
    Who turn a monster loose among mankind,   320
    Fiercer than famine, war, or spotted pestilence,

299. hunt] *Q, Op, Sp;* haunt *D2.*   wild and forgiving fiend! *Q;* wild
315. and unforgiving fiend!] *D2;*   unforgiving fiend!*Op, Sp.*

---

316. *undistinguished*] purposeless, haphazard.

Baneful as death and horrible as hell.

ALICIA.

If thou wilt curse, curse rather thine own falsehood;
Curse the lewd maxims of thy perjured sex,
Which taught thee first to laugh at faith and justice, 325
To scorn the solemn sanctity of oaths,
And make a jest of a poor woman's ruin;
Curse thy proud heart, and thy insulting tongue
That raised this fatal fury in my soul
And urged my vengeance to undo us both.   330

LORD HASTINGS.

Oh, thou inhuman! turn thy eyes away,
And blast me not with their destructive beams.
Why should I curse thee with my dying breath?
Begone! and let me sigh it out in peace.

ALICIA.

Canst thou, O cruel Hastings, leave me thus?   335
Hear me, I beg thee—I conjure thee, hear me!
While with an agonizing heart, I swear
By all the pangs I feel, by all the sorrows,
The terrors and despair thy loss shall give me,
My hate was on my rival bent alone.   340
Oh! had I once divined, false as thou art,
A danger to thy life, I would have died,
I would have met it for thee, and made bare
My ready, faithful breast to save thee from it.

LORD HASTINGS.

Now mark! and tremble at heav'ns just award.   345
While thy insatiate wrath and fell revenge
Pursued the innocence which never wronged thee,
Behold! the mischief falls on thee and me.
Remorse and heaviness of heart shall wait thee,
And everlasting anguish be thy potion;   350
For me, the snares of death are wound about me,
And now, in one poor moment, I am gone.
Oh! if thou hast one tender thought remaining,
Fly to thy closet, fall upon thy knee,

350. potion] *Q, D2, Op;* portion *Sp.*

351. *snares of death*] See Psalm 116:3: "The sorrows of death compassed me."

And recommend my parting soul to mercy.   355
ALICIA *(kneeling).*

Oh! yet, before I go forever from thee,
Turn thee in gentleness and pity to me,
And in compassion of my strong affliction,
Say, is it possible you can forgive
The fatal rashness of ungoverned love?   360
For oh! 'tis certain, if I had not loved thee
Beyond my peace, my reason, fame, and life,
Desired to death, and doted to distraction,
This day of horror never should have known us.

LORD HASTINGS *(raising her).*

Oh, rise, and let me hush thy stormy sorrows!   365
Assuage thy tears, for I will chide no more,
No more upbraid thee, thou unhappy fair one.
I see the hand of heav'n is armed against me,
And, in mysterious providence, decrees
To punish me by thy mistaking hand.   370
Most righteous doom! for, oh, while I behold thee,
Thy wrongs rise up in terrible array,
And charge thy ruin on me—thy fair fame,
Thy spotless beauty, innocence, and youth,
Dishonored, blasted, and betrayed by me!   375

ALICIA.

And does thy heart relent for my undoing?
Oh, that inhuman Gloster could be moved
But half so easily as I can pardon!

LORD HASTINGS.

Here, then, exchange we mutually forgiveness.
So may the guilt of all my broken vows,   380
My perjuries to thee, be all forgotten,
As here my soul acquits thee of my death,
As here I part without one angry thought,
As here I leave thee with the softest tenderness,
Mourning the chance of our disastrous loves,   385

384. thee] *D2, Op, Sp; Q omits.*

---

354. *fly to thy closet*] See Matthew 6:6: "But thou, when thou prayest,
enter into thy closet, and when thou has shut thy door, pray to thy Father
which is in secret; and thy Father which seeth in secret shall reward
thee openly."

And begging heav'n to bless and to support thee.

RATCLIFFE.

My lord, dispatch; the duke has sent to chide me
For loitering in my duty.

LORD HASTINGS.   I obey.

ALICIA.

Insatiate, savage, monster! Is a moment
So tedious to thy malice? Oh, repay him,   390
Thou great avenger; give him blood for blood!
Guilt haunt him! fiends pursue him! lightnings blast
    him!
Some horrid, cursed kind of death o'ertake him,
Sudden, and in fullness of his sins!
That he may know how terrible it is   395
To want that moment he denies thee now.

LORD HASTINGS.

'Tis all in vain, this rage that tears thy bosom;
Like a poor bird that flutters in its cage,
Thou beat'st thyself to death. Retire, I beg thee;
To see thee thus, thou know'st not how it wounds me;   400
Thy agonies are added to my own,
And make the burden more than I can bear.
Farewell! Good angels visit thy afflictions
And bring thee peace and comfort from above.

ALICIA.

Oh, stab me to the heart, some pitying hand   405
Now strike me dead—!

LORD HASTINGS.   One thing I had forgot—
I charge thee by our present common miseries,
By our past loves, if yet they have a name,
By all thy hopes of peace here and hereafter,
Let not the rancor of thy hate pursue   410
The innocence of thy unhappy friend.
Thou know'st who 'tis I mean; oh, shouldst thou wrong
    her,

389. savage] *Sp;* *Q, D2, Op*   405. hand] hand, *Q, D2, Op, Sp.*
capitalize (to indicate a noun).

---

394. *fullness of his sins*] See *Hamlet,* III.iv.81.
395–396. *That . . . now*] See *King Lear,* I.iv.309–311.
403. *Good angels visit*] See *Hamlet,* V.ii.370–371.

Just heav'n shall double all thy woes upon thee,
And make 'em know no end. Remember this
As the last warning of a dying man.   415
Farewell forever!   *The Guards carry* Hastings *off.*
ALICIA.   Forever! oh, forever!
Oh, who can bear to be a wretch forever!
My rival too! His last thoughts hung on her,
And, as he parted, left a blessing for her,
Shall she be blest, and I be curst, forever?   420
No! Since her fatal beauty was the cause
Of all my suff'rings, let her share my pains;
Let her, like me, of ev'ry joy forlorn,
Devote the hour when such a wretch was born:
Like me to deserts and to darkness run,   425
Abhor the day, and curse the golden sun;
Cast ev'ry good, and ev'ry hope behind;
Detest the works of nature, loathe mankind;
Like me, with cries distracted fill the air, ⎫
Tear her poor bosom, rend her frantic hair, ⎬   430
And prove the torments of the last despair. ⎭   *Exit.*

End of the Fourth Act

---

424. *Devote*] Curse.

ACT V

The street.
Enter Bellmour *and* Dumont, *or* Shore.

SHORE.
    You saw her then?
BELLMOUR.   I met her, as returning
In solemn penance from the public cross.
Before her, certain rascal officers,
Slaves in authority, the knaves of justice,
Proclaimed the tyrant Gloster's cruel orders.   5
On either side her marched an ill-looked priest,
Who with severe, with horrid, haggard eyes,
Did ever and anon by turns upbraid her,
And thunder in her trembling ear damnation.
Around her, numberless the rabble flowed,   10
Should'ring each other, crowding for a view,
Gaping and gazing, taunting and reviling;
Some pitying, but those, alas! how few!
The most, such iron-hearts we are, and such
The base barbarity of human kind,   15
With insolence and lewd reproach pursued her,
Hooting and railing, and with villainous hands
Gathering the filth from out the common ways,
To hurl upon her head.
SHORE.   Inhuman dogs!
How did she bear it?
BELLMOUR.   With the gentlest patience,   20
Submissive, sad, and lowly was her look;
A burning taper in her hand she bore,
And on her shoulders, carelessly confused,
With loose neglect her lovely tresses hung;
Upon her cheek a faintish flush was spread;   25
Feeble she seemed, and sorely smit with pain,

---

2. *solemn penance*] A similar sentence is passed on Eleanor Cobham, Duchess of Gloucester, in *2 Henry VI,* II.iii.9–12. The passage recalls Scroop's description of the procession of Richard II in *2 Henry IV,* I.iii.103–105.
   18. *the common ways*] public ditches, sewers.

While barefoot as she trod the flinty pavement,
Her footsteps all along were marked with blood.
Yet silent still she passed; and unrepining
Her streaming eyes bent ever on the earth,   30
Except when in some bitter pang of sorrow
To heav'n she seemed in fervent zeal to raise,
And beg that mercy man denied her here.

SHORE.
When was this piteous sight?

BELLMOUR.   These last two days.
You know my care was wholly bent on you,   35
To find the happy means of your deliverance,
Which but for Hastings' death I had not gained.
During that time, although I have not seen her,
Yet divers trusty messengers I've sent
To wait about and watch a fit convenience   40
To give her some relief; but all in vain.
A churlish guard attends upon her steps,
Who menace those with death that bring her comfort
And drive all succor from her.

SHORE.   Let 'em threaten.
Let proud oppression prove its fiercest malice;   45
So heav'n befriend my soul, as here I vow
To give her help and share one fortune with her.

BELLMOUR.
Mean you to see her thus, in your own form?

SHORE.
I do.

BELLMOUR. And have you thought upon the consequence?

SHORE.
What is there I should fear?

BELLMOUR.   Have you examined   50
Into your inmost heart, and tried at leisure
The several secret springs that move the passions?
Has mercy fixed her empire there so sure,
That wrath and vengeance never may return?
Can you resume a husband's name, and bid   55
That wakeful dragon, fierce resentment, sleep?

32. raise] *Q, Op, Sp;* raise them *(one copy of D2, according to Sutherland).*

SHORE.

    Why dost thou search so deep, and urge my memory
    To conjure up my wrongs to life again?
    I have long labored to forget myself,
    To think on all time, backward, like a space   60
    Idle and void, where nothing e'er had being.
    But thou hast peopled it again; revenge
    And jealousy renew their horrid forms,
    Shoot all their fires, and drive me to distraction.

BELLMOUR.

    Far be the thought from me! my care was only   65
    To arm you for the meeting. Better were it
    Never to see her again than to let that name
    Recall forgotten rage, and make the husband
    Destroy the generous pity of Dumont.

SHORE.

    Oh! thou hast set my busy brain at work,   70
    And now she musters up a train of images
    Which to preserve my peace I had cast aside
    And sunk to deep oblivion. —Oh, that form!
    That angel-face on which my dotage hung!
    How I have gazed upon her, till my soul   75
    With very eagerness went forth towards her,
    And issued at my eyes. Was there a gem
    Which the sun ripens in the Indian mine,
    Or the rich bosom of the ocean yields—
    What was there art could make, or wealth could buy,   80
    Which I have left unsought to deck her beauty?
    What could her king do more?—And yet she fled.

BELLMOUR.

    Away with that sad fancy.

SHORE.   Oh, that day!

    The thought of it must live forever with me.
    I met her, Bellmour, when the royal spoiler   85
    Bore her in triumph from my widowed home!
    Within his chariot by his side she sate

---

87. she] *D2, Op, Sp;* he *Q.*

77–79. *gem . . . yields*] the diamond and the pearl; Shore was a jeweler
and goldsmith.

And listened to his talk with downward looks,
Till sudden, as she chanced aside to glance,
Her eyes encountered mine. —Oh, then, my friend!   90
Oh, who can paint my grief and her amazement!
As at the stroke of death, twice turned she pale,
And twice a burning crimson blushed all o'er her;
Then, with a shriek heart-wounding, loud she cried,
While down her cheeks two gushing torrents ran   95
Fast falling on her hands, which thus she wrung.
Moved at her grief, the tyrant ravisher
With courteous action wooed her oft to turn;
Earnest he seemed to plead, but all in vain;
Ev'n to the last she bent her sight towards me,   100
And followed me—till I had lost myself.

BELLMOUR.

Alas, for pity! Oh, those speaking tears!
Could they be false? Did she not suffer with you?
And though the king by force possessed her person,
Her unconsenting heart dwelt still with you.   105
If all her former woes were not enough,
Look on her now; behold her where she wanders,
Hunted to death, distressed on every side,
With no one hand to help; and tell me, then,
If ever misery were known like hers.   110

SHORE.

And can she bear it? Can that delicate frame
Endure the beating of a storm so rude?
Can she, for whom the various seasons changed
To court her appetite and crown her board,
For whom the foreign vintages were pressed,   115
For whom the merchant spread his silken stores,
Can she—
Entreat for bread, and want the needful raiment
To wrap her shivering bosom from the weather?
When she was mine, no care came ever nigh her.   120
I thought the gentlest breeze that wakes the spring
Too rough to breathe upon her. Cheerfulness
Danced all the day before her, and at night

91. paint] *Op;* point *Q, D2, Sp.*   94. shriek] *Sp;* skriek *Q, D2, Op.*

Soft slumbers waited on her downy pillow.
Now sad and shelterless, perhaps, she lies   125
Where piercing winds blow sharp, and the chill rain
Drops from some penthouse on her wretched head,
Drenches her locks, and kills her with the cold.
It is too much. —Hence with her past offenses;
They are atoned at full. Why stay we then?   130
Oh! let us haste, my friend, and find her out.

BELLMOUR.

Somewhere about this quarter of the town,
I hear the poor, abandoned creature lingers.
Her guard, though set with strictest watch to keep
All food and friendship from her, yet permit her   135
To wander the streets, there choose her bed,
And rest her head on what cold stone she pleases.

SHORE.

Here let us then divide, each in his round
To search her sorrows out. Whose hap it is
First to behold her, this way let him lead   140
Her fainting steps, and meet we here together.   *Exeunt.*

Enter Jane Shore, *her hair hanging loose on her shoulders, and
barefooted.*

JANE SHORE.

Yet, yet endure, nor murmur, O my soul!
For are not thy transgressions great and numberless?
Do not they cover thee, like rising floods,
And press thee like a weight of waters down?   145
Does not the hand of righteousness afflict thee;
And who shall plead against it? Who shall say
To pow'r almighty, "Thou hast done enough"
Or bid his dreadful rod of vengeance stay?
Wait then with patience till the circling hours   150
Shall bring the time of thy appointed rest
And lay thee down in death. The hireling thus
With labor drudges out the painful day,
And often looks with long expecting eyes
To see the shadows rise and be dismissed.   155
And hark! methinks the roar that late pursued me

---

127. *penthouse*] a sloping roof or overhanging shed.

Sinks like the murmurs of a falling wind,
And softens into silence. Does revenge
And malice then grow weary, and forsake me?
My guard, too, that observed me still so close,   160
Tire in the task of their inhuman office,
And loiter far behind. Alas! I faint,
My spirits fail at once. —This is the door
Of my Alicia—blessed opportunity!
I'll steal a little succor from her goodness   165
Now, while no eye observes me.   *She knocks at the door.*

Enter a Servant.

                                   Is your lady,
My gentle friend, at home? Oh, bring me to her. *Going in.*
SERVANT *(putting her back).*
    Hold, mistress, whither would you?
JANE SHORE.   Do you not know me?
SERVANT.
    I know you well, and know my orders too.
    You must not enter here.
JANE SHORE.   Tell my Alicia,   170
    'Tis I would see her.
SERVANT.   She is ill at ease
    And will admit no visitor.
JANE SHORE.   But tell her
    'Tis I, her friend, the partner of her heart,
    Wait at the door and beg—
SERVANT.   'Tis all in vain.
    Go hence, and howl to those that will regard you.   175
                                   Shuts the door, and exit.
JANE SHORE.
    It was not always thus; the time has been
    When this unfriendly door that bars my passage
    Flew wide, and almost leaped from off its hinges
    To give me entrance here; when this good house
    Has poured forth all its dwellers to receive me;   180
    When my approach has made a little holy-day,
    And ev'ry face was dressed in smiles to meet me.
    But now 'tis otherwise, and those who blessed me
    Now curse me to my face. Why should I wander,

Stray further on, for I can die ev'n here!   185

She sits down at the door.

Enter Alicia *in disorder, two* Servants *following.*

ALICIA.

    What wretch art thou whose misery and baseness
    Hangs on my doors; whose hateful whine of woe
    Breaks in upon my sorrows, and distracts
    My jarring senses with thy beggar's cry?

JANE SHORE.

    A very beggar, and a wretch indeed;   190
    One driv'n by strong calamity to seek
    For succor here; one perishing for want,
    Whose hunger has not tasted food these three days;
    And humbly asks, for charity's dear sake,
    A draught of water and a little bread.   195

ALICIA.

    And dost thou come to me, to me for bread?
    I know thee not. Go, hunt for it abroad,
    Where wanton hands upon the earth have scattered it,
    Or cast it on the waters. —Mark the eagle
    And hungry vulture, where they wind the prey;   200
    Watch where the ravens of the valley feed,
    And seek thy food with them—I know thee not.

JANE SHORE.

    And yet there was a time when my Alicia
    Has thought unhappy Shore her dearest blessing,
    And mourned the livelong day she passed without me;   205
    When, paired like turtles, we were still together;
    When often as we prattled arm in arm,
    Inclining fondly to me, she has sworn
    She loved me more than all the world beside.

ALICIA.

    Ha! say'st thou! Let me look upon thee well.   210
    'Tis true—I know thee now— A mischief on thee!
    Thou art that fatal fair, that cursed she,

---

200. *wind*] to scent.

201. *ravens of the valley*] Elijah the Tishbite was fed by ravens at the brook Cherith; see I Kings 17:4–6. See also Proverbs 30:17.

206. *turtles*] turtle doves.

That set my brain a madding. Thou hast robbed me;
Thou hast undone me. —Murder! Oh, my Hastings!
See, his pale, bloody head shoots glaring by me!   215
Give him me back again, thou soft deluder,
Thou beauteous witch—

JANE SHORE.   Alas, I never wronged you!
Oh, then be good to me; have pity on me!
Thou never knew'st the bitterness of want,
And mayst thou never know it. Oh, bestow   220
Some poor remain, the voiding of thy table,
A morsel to support my famished soul.

ALICIA.

Avaunt! and come not near me—

JANE SHORE.   To thy hand
I trusted all, gave my whole store to thee.
Nor do I ask it back; allow me but   225
The smallest pittance, give me but to eat,
Lest I fall down and perish here before thee.

ALICIA.

Nay, tell not me! Where is thy king, thy Edward,
And all the smiling, cringing train of courtiers
That bent the knee before thee?

JANE SHORE.   Oh, for mercy!   230

ALICIA.

Mercy? I know it not—for I am miserable.
I'll give thee misery, for here she dwells.
This is her house, where the sun never dawns,
The bird of night sits screaming o'er the roof,
Grim spectres sweep along the horrid gloom,   235
And nought is heard but wailings and lamentings.
Hark! something cracks above!—It shakes, it totters!
And see, the nodding ruin falls to crush me!
'Tis fall'n, 'tis here! I feel it on my brain!

FIRST SERVANT.

This sight disorders her.

SECOND SERVANT.   Retire, dear lady,   240
And leave this woman—

---

213. *a madding*] raving.
224. *my whole store*] the casket of jewels; see I.ii.156–163, above.
234. *bird of night*] the owl.

ALICIA.   Let her take my counsel!
    Why shouldst thou be a wretch? Stab, tear thy heart,
    And rid thyself of this detested being;
    I wo'not linger long behind thee here.
    A waving flood of bluish fire swells o'er me;   245
    And now 'tis out, and I am drowned in blood.
    Ha! what art thou, thou horrid headless trunk?
    It is my Hastings!—See, he wafts me on!—
    Away! I go! I fly! I follow thee.—
    But come not thou with mischief-making beauty   250
    To interpose between us; look not on him;
    Give thy fond arts and thy delusions o'er,
    For thou shalt never, never part us more.
                            She runs off, her Servants *following.*
JANE SHORE.
    Alas! She raves; her brain, I fear, is turned.
    In mercy look upon her, gracious heaven,   **255**
    Nor visit her for any wrong to me.
    Sure, I am near upon my journey's end;
    My head runs round, my eyes begin to fail,
    And dancing shadows swim before my sight.
    I can no more. *(Lies down.)*   Receive me, thou cold
        earth;   260
    Thou common parent, take me to thy bosom,
    And let me rest with thee.

                    Enter Bellmour.

BELLMOUR.   Upon the ground!
    Thy miseries can never lay thee lower.—
    Look up, thou poor afflicted one! thou mourner,
    Whom none has comforted! Where are thy friends, 265
    The dear companions of thy joyful days,
    Whose hearts thy warm prosperity made glad,
    Whose arms were taught to grow like ivy round thee
    And bind thee to their bosoms? "Thus with thee,
    Thus let us live, and let us die," they said,   270
    "For sure thou art the sister of our loves,
    And nothing shall divide us."—Now where are they?

255. heaven] *Q, Op, Sp;* heav'n *D2.*

JANE SHORE.

    Ah! Bellmour, where indeed! They stand aloof,
    And view my desolation from afar;
    When they pass by, they shake their heads in scorn 275
    And cry, "Behold the harlot and her end!"
    And yet thy goodness turns aside to pity me!
    Alas! there may be danger; get thee gone!
    Let me not pull a ruin on thy head!
    Leave me to die alone, for I am fall'n   280
    Never to rise, and all relief is vain.

BELLMOUR.

    Yet raise thy drooping head, for I am come
    To chase away despair. Behold, where yonder
    That honest man, that faithful, brave Dumont,
    Is hastening to thy aid!

JANE SHORE.   Dumont? Ha! where?   285

                   Raising herself and looking about.
    Then heav'n has heard my pray'r; his very name
    Renews the springs of life and cheers my soul.
    Has he then 'scaped the snare?

BELLMOUR.   He has: but see—

    He comes, unlike to that Dumont you knew,
    For now he wears your better angel's form,   290
    And comes to visit you with peace and pardon.

               Enter Shore.

JANE SHORE.

    Speak, tell me! Which is he? And oh! what would
    This dreadful vision! See, it comes upon me—
    It is my husband—Ah!   *She swoons.*

SHORE.   She faints! Support her!

    Sustain her head while I infuse this cordial   295
    Into her dying lips; from spicy drugs,
    Rich herbs, and flow'rs the potent juice is drawn;
    With wondrous force it strikes the lazy spirits,
    Drives 'em around, and wakens life anew.

BELLMOUR.

    Her weakness could not bear the strong surprise.   300
    But see, she stirs! and the returning blood

   295. *infuse*] pour.

68

Faintly begins to blush again, and kindle
Upon her ashy cheek—

SHORE *(raising her up).*   So—gently raise her—

JANE SHORE.

Ha! what art thou?—Bellmour!

BELLMOUR.   How fare you, lady?

JANE SHORE.

My heart is thrilled with horror—

BELLMOUR.   Be of courage;   305
Your husband lives! 'Tis he, my worthiest friend—

JANE SHORE.

Still art thou there? Still dost thou hover round me?
Oh, save me, Bellmour, from his angry shade!

BELLMOUR.

'Tis he himself! He lives! Look up—

JANE SHORE.   I dare not!
Oh, that my eyes could shut him out forever—   310

SHORE.

Am I so hateful then, so deadly to thee,
To blast thy eyes with horror? Since I'm grown
A burthen to the world, myself, and thee,
Would I had ne'er survived to see thee more.

JANE SHORE.

Oh, thou most injured! Dost thou live, indeed?   315
Fall, then, ye mountains, on my guilty head;
Hide me, ye rocks, within your secret caverns;
Cast thy black veil upon my shame, O night,
And shield me with thy sable wing forever!

SHORE.

Why dost thou turn away? Why tremble thus?   320
Why thus indulge thy fears, and in despair,
Abandon thy distracted soul to horror?
Cast every black and guilty thought behind thee,
And let 'em never vex thy quiet more.
My arms, my heart are open to receive thee,   325
To bring thee back to thy forsaken home
With tender joy, with fond, forgiving love,

---

316. *Fall, then, ye mountains*] The Day of Wrath or Judgment; see Hosea
10:8; Luke 23:30; Revelation 6:15–17.

317. *Hide me, ye rocks*] Revelation 6:15.

And all the longings of my first desires.

JANE SHORE.

No, arm thy brow with vengeance, and appear
The minister of heav'n's enquiring justice;   330
Array thyself all terrible for judgment,
Wrath in thy eyes, and thunder in thy voice;
Pronounce my sentence, and if yet there be
A woe I have not felt, inflict it on me.

SHORE.

The measure of thy sorrows is complete,   335
And I am come to snatch thee from injustice.
The hand of pow'r no more shall crush thy weakness,
Nor proud oppression grind thy humble soul.

JANE SHORE.

Art thou not ris'n by miracle from death?
Thy shroud is fall'n from off thee, and the grave   340
Was bid to give thee up, that thou might'st come
The messenger of grace and goodness to me,
To seal my peace and bless me ere I go.
Oh, let me then fall down beneath thy feet
And weep my gratitude forever there;   345
Give my your drops, ye soft-descending rains,
Give me your streams, ye never-ceasing springs,
That my sad eyes may still supply my duty,
And feed an everlasting flood of sorrow.

SHORE.

Waste not thy feeble spirits. I have long   350
Beheld, unknown, thy mourning and repentance;
Therefore my heart has set aside the past,
And holds thee white as unoffending innocence;
Therefore, in spite of cruel Gloster's rage,
Soon as my friend had broke my prison doors,   355
I flew to thy assistance. Let us haste
Now, while occasion seems to smile upon us,
Forsake this place of shame and find a shelter.

JANE SHORE.

What shall I say to you? But I obey—

SHORE.

Lean on my arm—

JANE SHORE.   Alas! I am wondrous faint: 360

But that's not strange; I have not eat these three days.

SHORE.

Oh, merciless! Look here, my love, I've brought thee
Some rich conserves.

JANE SHORE.   How can you be so good?
But you were ever thus; I well remember
With what fond care, what diligence of love,   365
You lavished out your wealth to buy me pleasures,
Preventing every wish. Have you forgot
The costly string of pearls you brought me home
And tied about my neck? How could I leave you?

SHORE.

Taste some of this, or this—

JANE SHORE.   You're strangely altered— 370
Say, gentle Bellmour, is he not? How pale
Your visage is become! Your eyes are hollow;
Nay, you are wrinkled too. —Alas the day!
My wretchedness has cost you many a tear
And many a bitter pang since last we parted.   375

SHORE.

No more of that. —Thou talk'st but dost not eat.

JANE SHORE.

My feeble jaws forget their common office,
My tasteless tongue cleaves to the clammy roof,
And now a gen'ral loathing grows upon me.
Oh, I am sick at heart.

SHORE.   Thou murd'rous sorrow!   380
Wo't thou still drink her blood, pursue her still?
Must she then die? Oh, my poor penitent,
Speak peace to thy sad heart. —She hears me not;
Grief masters ev'ry sense. Help me to hold her—

            Enter Catesby, *with a Guard.*

CATESBY.

Seize on 'em both, as traitors to the state.   385

            Guard lays hold on Shore *and* Bellmour.

BELLMOUR.

What means this violence?

---

363. *conserves*] fruit jams.
367. *Preventing*] anticipating.

CATESBY.　　　　　　　　　Have we not found you,
　　In scorn of the Protector's strict command,
　　Assisting this base woman and abetting
　　Her infamy?
SHORE.　　　　　　Infamy on thy head!
　　Thou tool of power, thou pander to authority!　　　390
　　I tell thee, knave, thou know'st of none so virtuous,
　　And she that bore thee was an Ethiop to her!
CATESBY.
　　You'll answer this at full. —Away with 'em.
SHORE.
　　Is charity grown treason to your court?
　　What honest man would live beneath such rulers?　　　395
　　I am content that we shall die together.
CATESBY.
　　Convey the men to prison; but for her,
　　Leave her to hunt her fortune as she may.
JANE SHORE.
　　I will not part with him!—For me—for me!
　　Oh, must he die for me?
　　　　　　　　　Following him as he is carried off. She falls.
SHORE.　　　　　　　　Inhuman villains!　　　400
　　　　　　　　　　　　Breaks from the Guard.
　　Stand off! the agonies of death are on her.
　　She pulls, she gripes me hard with her cold hand.
JANE SHORE.
　　Was this blow wanting to complete my ruin?
　　Oh let him go, ye ministers of terror;
　　He shall offend no more, for I will die　　　405
　　And yield obedience to your cruel master.
　　Tarry a little, but a little longer,
　　And take my last breath with you.
SHORE.　　　　　　　　　　Oh my love!
　　Why have I lived to see this bitter moment,
　　This grief by far surpassing all my former!　　　410
　　Why dost thou fix thy dying eyes upon me
　　With such an earnest, such a piteous look,
　　As if thy heart were full of some sad meaning
　　Thou couldst not speak!
JANE SHORE.　　　　　　Forgive me!—but forgive me!

SHORE.

    Be witness for me, ye celestial host,   415
    Such mercy and such pardon as my soul
    Accords to thee, and begs of heav'n to show thee,
    May such befall me at my latest hour,
    And make my portion blest or curst forever.

JANE SHORE.

    Then all is well, and I shall sleep in peace.   420
    'Tis very dark, and I have lost you now.
    Was there not something I would have bequeathed
      you?
    But I have nothing left me to bestow,
    Nothing but one sad sigh. Oh, Mercy, heav'n!   *Dies.*

BELLMOUR.

    There fled the soul,   425
    And left her load of misery behind.

SHORE.

    Oh, my heart's treasure! Is this pale, sad visage
    All that remains of thee? Are these dead eyes
    The light that cheer my soul? Oh, heavy hour!
    But I will fix my trembling lips to thine   430
    Till I am cold and senseless quite, as thou art.
    What, must we part then?— *To the Guards taking him away.*
           Will you? *(Kissing her.)*   Fare thee well!
    Now execute your tyrant's will, and lead me
    To bonds or death, 'tis equally indifferent.

BELLMOUR.

    Let those who view this sad example know   435
    What fate attends the broken marriage vow;
    And teach their children in succeeding times,
    No common vengeance waits upon these crimes,
    When such severe repentance could not save,
    From want, from shame, and an untimely grave.
                     Exeunt.   440

FINIS

---

430. *But . . . thine*] See *Romeo and Juliet,* V.iii.164.

EPILOGUE

Spoken by Mrs. Oldfield

Ye modest matrons all, ye virtuous wives,
Who lead with horrid husbands decent lives,
You who, for all you are in such a taking ⎫
To see your spouses drinking, gaming, raking, ⎬
Yet make a conscience still of cuckold-making, ⎭ 5
What can we say your pardon to obtain?
This matter here was proved against poor Jane:
She never once denied it, but in short,
Whimpered, and cried, "Sweet sir, I'm sorry for't."
'Twas well she met a kind, good-natured soul; 10
We are not all so easy to control.
I fancy one might find in this good town
Some would ha' told the gentleman his own;
Have answered smart, "To what do you pretend,
Blockhead! As if I mustn't see a friend! 15
Tell me of hackney-coaches, jaunts to th' City,
Where should I buy my china— Faith, I'll fit ye!"
Our wife was of a milder, meeker spirit:
You! lords and masters! was not that some merit?
Don't you allow it to be virtuous bearing 20
When we submit thus to your domineering?
Well, peace be with her; she did wrong most surely,
But so do many more who look demurely.
Nor should our mourning madam weep alone,
There are more ways of wickedness than one. 25
If the reforming stage should fall to shaming
Ill-nature, pride, hypocrisy, and gaming,

0.1.] i.e., spoken in the character of Jane Shore.

3. *a taking*] agitation.

4. *raking*] whoring.

15–16. *musn't . . . City*] a reference to Mrs. Margery Pinchwife in William Wycherley's *The Country Wife* (1674–75).

17. *buy my china*] a reference to the notorious "china scene" in *The Country Wife*, IV.iii.

17. *I'll fit ye*] prepare you (for a pair of cuckhold horns).

26. *reforming stage*] a reference to the changing taste in the theaters following the Jeremy Collier controversy, which began in 1698.

74

The poets frequently might move compassion,
And with she-tragedies o'errun the nation.
Then judge the fair offender, with good nature;   30
And let your fellow-feeling curb your satire.
What if our neighbors have some little failing,
Must we needs fall to damning and to railing?
For her excuse, too, be it understood,   ⎫
That if the woman was not quite so good,   ⎬   35
Her lover was a king, she flesh and blood.   ⎭
And since she has dearly paid the sinful score,
Be kind at last, and pity poor Jane Shore.

34. excuse,too] excuse too, *Q, D2,*
Op, Sp.

---

29. *she-tragedies*] Rowe's own term for the sentimental-pathetic
tragedies with female protagonists.

Appendix A

Shakespeare's *The Tragedy of Richard III*
Act III, Scene iv

The text below is taken from J. Dover Wilson, ed., *The New Shakespeare* (Cambridge: Cambridge University Press, 1954), pp. 71–75. Used with the kind permission of the publishers.

A room in the Tower of London. Buckingham, Stanley, Hastings, the Bishop of Ely, Ratcliffe, Lovel, *with others, at a table.*

HASTINGS.

    Now, noble peers, the cause why we are met
    Is to determine of the coronation.
    In God's name, speak! when is the royal day?

BUCKINGHAM.

    Is all things ready for the royal time?

STANLEY.

    It is, and wants but nomination.   5

ELY.

    To-morrow then I judge a happy day.

BUCKINGHAM.

    Who knows the Lord Protector's mind herein?
    Who is most inward with the noble duke?

ELY.

    Your grace, we think, should soonest know his mind.

BUCKINGHAM.

    We know each other's faces: for our hearts,   10
    He knows no more of mine than I of yours;
    Or I of his, my lord, than you of mine.
    Lord Hastings, you and he are near in love.

HASTINGS.

    I thank his grace, I know he loves me well;
    But, for his purpose in the coronation,   15

I have not sounded him, nor he delivered
His gracious pleasure any way therein:
But you, my honourable lords, may name the time;
And in the duke's behalf I'll give my voice,
Which, I presume, he'll take in gentle part.   20

[*Enter* Gloucester.]

ELY.

In happy time, here comes the duke himself.

GLOUSTER.

My noble lords and cousins all, good morrow.
I have been long a sleeper; but I trust
My absence doth neglect no great design,
Which by my presence might have been concluded.   25

BUCKINGHAM.

Had you not come upon your cue, my lord,
William Lord Hastings had pronounced your part—
I mean, your voice for crowning of the king.

GLOUCESTER.

Than my Lord Hastings no man might be bolder;
His lordship knows me well, and loves me well.   30
My lord of Ely, when I was last in Holborn,
I saw good strawberries in your garden there:
I do beseech you send for some of them.

ELY.

Marry, and will, my lord, with all my heart.   *He goes.*

GLOUCESTER.

Cousin of Buckingham, a word with you. *Drawing him aside.* 35
Catesby hath sounded Hastings in our business,
And finds the testy gentleman so hot,
That he will lose his head ere give consent
His master's child, as worshipfully he terms it,
Shall lose the royalty of England's throne.   40

BUCKINGHAM.

Withdraw yourself a while, I'll go with you.   *They go out.*

STANLEY.

We have not yet set down this day of triumph.
To-morrow, in my judgement, is too sudden;
For I myself am not so well provided
As else I would be, were the day prolonged.   45

The Bishop of Ely *returns.*

ELY.

Where is my Lord the Duke of Gloucester?
I have sent for these strawberries.

HASTINGS.

His grace looks cheerfully and smooth this morning;
There's some conceit or other likes him well,
When that he bids good-morrow with such spirit.　　50
I think there's ne'er a man in Christendom
Can lesser hide his love or hate than he;
For by his face straight shall you know his heart.

STANLEY.

What of his heart perceive you in his face
By any livelihood he showed to-day?　　55

HASTINGS.

Marry, that with no man here he is offended;
For, were he, he had shown it in his looks.

Gloucester *and* Buckingham *return;* Gloucester *with a wonderful
sour countenance, knitting his brow and gnawing his lip.*

GLOUCESTER.

I pray you all, tell me what they deserve
That do conspire my death with devilish plots
Of damnéd witchcraft, and that have prevailed　　60
Upon my body with their hellish charms?

HASTINGS.

The tender love I bear your grace, my lord,
Makes me most forward in this princely presence
To doom th'offenders: whosoe'er they be,
I say, my lord, they have deservéd death.　　65

GLOUCESTER.

Then be your eyes the witness of their evil.
Look how I am bewitched; behold, mine arm
Is like a blasted sapling withered up:
And this is Edward's wife, that monstrous witch,
Consorted with that harlot, strumpet Shore,　　70
That by their witchcraft thus have markéd me.

HASTINGS.

If they have done this deed, my noble lord,—

GLOUCESTER.

> If! thou protector of this damnéd strumpet,
> Talk'st thou to me of "ifs"? Thou art a traitor:
> Off with his head! Now, by Saint Paul I swear, 75
> I will not dine until I see the same.
> Lovel and Ratcliffe, look that it be done:
> The rest that love me, rise and follow me.
>
> > *All leave but* Hastings, Ratcliffe *and* Lovel.

HASTINGS.

> Woe, woe for England! not a whit for me;
> For I, too fond, might have prevented this. 80
> Stanley did dream the boar did raze our helms,
> And I did scorn it, and disdain to fly:
> Three times to-day my foot-cloth horse did stumble,
> And started when he looked upon the Tower,
> As loath to bear me to the slaughter-house. 85
> O, now I need the priest that spake to me:
> I now repent I told the pursuivant,
> As too triumphing, how mine enemies
> To-day at Pomfret bloodily were butchered,
> And I myself secure in grace and favour. 90
> O Margaret, Margaret, now thy heavy curse
> Is lighted on poor Hastings' wretched head!

RATCLIFFE.

> Come, come, dispatch; the duke would be at dinner:
> Make a short shrift; he longs to see your head.

HASTINGS.

> O momentary grace of mortal men, 95
> Which we more hunt for than the grace of God!
> Who builds his hope in air of your good looks
> Lives like a drunken sailor on a mast,
> Ready with every nod to tumble down
> Into the fatal bowels of the deep. 100

LOVEL.

> Come, come, dispatch; 'tis bootless to exclaim.

HASTINGS.

> O bloody Richard! miserable England!
> I prophesy the fearfull'st time to thee
> That ever wretched age hath looked upon.
> Come, lead me to the block; bear him my head. 105
> They smile at me who shortly shall be dead. *He is led away.*

Appendix B

The Ballad of The Woeful Lamentation of Jane Shore

The text below is taken from *Percy's Reliques of Ancient English Poetry,* ed. M. M. Arnold Schroer (Berlin, 1893), I, 431–435.

The Woeful Lamentation of Jane Shore,
A Goldsmith's Wife in London,
Sometime King Edward IV his Concubine

(To the tune of *Live with me,* &)

To every stanza is annexed the following burden:

Then maids and wives in time amend,
For love and beauty will have end.

If Rosamond that was so fair,
Had cause her sorrows to declare,
Then let Jane Shore with sorrow sing   5
That was beloved of a king.

In maiden years my beauty bright
Was loved dear of lord and knight;
But yet the love that they required,
It was not as my friends desired.   10

My parents they, for thirst of gain,
A husband for me did obtain;
And I, their pleasure to fulfill,
Was forced to wed against my will.

To Matthew Shore I was a wife,   15

---

3. *Rosamond*] Fair Rosamond, mistress of Henry II, herself the subject of an old ballad.

15. *Matthew Shore*] so called in most accounts, but the given name was William (see Harl. MSS. 433, Article 2378, letter of Richard III to the Bishop of Lincoln, Lord Chancellor, 1484.)

Till lust brought ruin to my life;
And then my life I lewdly spent,
Which makes my soul for to lament.

In Lombard-street I once did dwell,
As London yet can witness well;   20
Where many gallants did behold
My beauty in a shop of gold.

I spread my plumes, as wantons do,
Some sweet and secret friends to woo,
Because chaste love I did not find   25
Agreeing to my wanton mind.

At last my name in court did ring
Into the ears of England's king,
Who came and liked, and love required,
But I made coy what he desired: 30

Yet Mistress Blague, a neighbor near,
Whose friendship I esteemed dear,
Did say, It was a gallant thing
To be beloved of a king.

By her persuasions I was led   35
For to defile my marriage-bed,
And wrong my wedded husband Shore,
Whom I had married years before.

In heart and mind I did rejoice,
That I had made so sweet a choice;   40
And therefore did my state resign,
To be king Edward's concubine.

From city then to court I went,
To reap the pleasures of content;
There had the joys that love could bring,   45
And knew the secrets of a king.

When I was thus advanced on high,
Commanding Edward with mine eye,
For Mrs. Blague I in short space

---

30. *made coy*] declined modestly.
31. *Mistress Blague*] according to tradition a lace-woman to the Court
who served as a bawd and entertained the masqued Edward IV and
Jane Shore. She becomes the Alicia of Rowe's drama.

Obtained a living from his grace. 50

No friends I had but in short time
I made unto a promotion climb;
But yet for all this costly pride,
My husband could not me abide.

His bed, though wronged by a king, 55
His heart with deadly grief did sting;
From England then he goes away
To end his life beyond the sea.

He could not live to see his name
Impaired by my wanton shame; 60
Although a prince of peerless might
Did reap the pleasure of his right.

Long time I lived in the court,
With lords and ladies of great sort;
And when I smiled all men were glad, 65
But when I frowned my prince grew sad.

But yet a gentle mind I bore
To helpless people, that were poor;
I still redrest the orphan's cry,
And saved their lives condemned to die. 70

I still had ruth on widows' tears,
I succored babes of tender years;
And never looked for other gain
But love and thanks for all my pain.

At last my royal king did die, 75
And then my days of woe grew nigh;
When crook-back Richard got the crown,
King Edward's friends were soon put down.

I then was punished for my sin,
That I so long had lived in; 80
Yes, every one that was his friend,
This tyrant brought to shameful end.

Then for my lewd and wanton life,

---

50. *a living*] an estate valued at £1200 a year.
58. *beyond the sea*] Some accounts say Shore returned and died a poor man in the reign of Henry VII.

That made a strumpèt of a wife,
I penance did in Lombard-street,   85
In shameful manner in a sheet.

Where many thousands did me view,
Who late in court my credit knew;
Which made the tears run down my face,
To think upon my foul disgrace.   90

Not thus content, they took from me
My goods, my livings, and my fee,
And charged that none should me relieve,
Nor any succor to me give.

Then unto Mrs. Blague I went,   95
To whom my jewels I had sent,
In hope thereby to ease my want,
When riches failed, and love grew scant:

But she denied to me the same
When in my need for them I came;   100
To recompence my former love,
Out of her doors she did me shove.

So love did vanish with my state,
Which now my soul repents too late;
Therefore example take by me,   105
For friendship parts in poverty.

But yet one friend among the rest,
Whom I before had seen distrest,
And saved his life, condemned to die,
Did give me food to succor me: 110

For which, by law, it was decreed
That he was hanged for that deed;
His death did grieve me so much more,
Than had I died myself therefore.

Then those to whom I had done good   115
Durst not afford me any food;
Whereby I begged all the day,

---

85. *penance*] See *Jane Shore*, V.1–33.
96. *my jewels*] See *Jane Shore*, I.ii.156–163.
107–114.] Tradition has it that a baker was hanged for throwing out a penny-loaf to her.

And still in streets by night I lay.

My gowns beset with pearl and gold,
Were turned to simple garments old;   120
My chains and gems and golden rings,
To filthy rags and loathsome things.

Thus was I scorned of maid and wife,
For leading such a wicked life;
Both suckling babes and children small,   125
Did make their pastime at my fall.

I could not get one bit of bread,
Whereby my hunger might be fed:
Nor drink, but such as channels yield,
Or stinking ditches in the field.   130

Thus, weary of my life, at length
I yielded up my vital strength,
Within a ditch of loathsome scent,
Where carrion dogs did much frequent:

The which now since my dying day,   135
Is Shoreditch called, as writers say;
Which is a witness of my sin,
For being concubine to a king.

You wanton wives, that fall to lust,
Be you assured that God is just;   140
Whoredom shall not escape his hand,
Nor pride unpunished in this land.

If God to me such shame did bring,
That yielded only to a king,
How shall they 'scape that daily run   145
To practice sin with every one?

You husbands, match not but for love,
Lest some disliking after prove;
Women, be warned when you are wives,
What plagues are due to sinful lives: 150
    Then maids and wives in time amend,
    For love and beauty will have end.

---

129. *channels*] public sewage ditches.
136. *Shoreditch*] a suburban district of London, existing much earlier
than the time of Jane Shore.

Appendix C

Chronology

Approximate dates are indicated by*. Dates for plays are those on which they were first made public, either on stage or in print.

Political and Literary Events	*Life and Major Works of Rowe*
1631	
Death of Donne.	
John Dryden born.	
1633	
Samuel Pepys born.	
1635	
Sir George Etherege born.*	
1640	
Aphra Behn born.*	
1641	
William Wycherley born.*	
1642	
First Civil War began (ended 1646).	
Theaters closed by Parliament.	
Thomas Shadwell born.*	
1648	
Second Civil War.	
Nathaniel Lee born.*	
1649	
Execution of Charles I.	
1650	
Jeremy Collier born.	
1651	
Hobbes's *Leviathan* published.	
1652	
First Dutch War began (ended 1654).	

Thomas Otway born.

1656

D'Avenant's *THE SIEGE OF RHODES* performed at Rutland House.

1657

John Dennis born.

1658

Death of Oliver Cromwell.

D'Avenant's *THE CRUELTY OF THE SPANIARDS IN PERU* performed at the Cockpit.

1660

Restoration of Charles II.

Theatrical patents granted to Thomas Killigrew and Sir William D'Avenant, authorizing them to form, repectively, the King's and the Duke of York's Companies.

Pepys began his diary.

1661

Cowley's *THE CUTTER OF COLE-MAN STREET*.

D'Avenant's *THE SIEGE OF RHODES* (expanded to two parts).

1662

Charter granted to the Royal Society.

1663

Dryden's *THE WILD GALLANT*.

Tuke's *THE ADVENTURES OF FIVE HOURS*.

1664

Sir John Vanbrugh born.

Dryden's *THE RIVAL LADIES*.

Dryden and Howard's *THE INDIAN QUEEN*.

Etherege's *THE COMICAL RE-VENGE*.

1665

Second Dutch War began (ended 1667).

Great Plague.

Dryden's *THE INDIAN EMPEROR*.

Orrery's *MUSTAPHA*.

1666

Fire of London.

Death of James Shirley.

1667

Jonathan Swift born.

Milton's *Paradise Lost* published.

Sprat's *The History of the Royal Society* published.

Dryden's *SECRET LOVE*.

1668

Death of D'Avenant.

Dryden made Poet Laureate.

Dryden's *An Essay of Dramatic Poesy* published.

Shadwell's *THE SULLEN LOVERS*.

Etherege's *SHE WOULD IF SHE COULD*.

1669

Pepys terminated his diary.

Susanna Centlivre born.

1670

William Congreve born.

Dryden's *THE CONQUEST OF GRANADA*, Part I.

1671

Dorset Garden Theatre (Duke's Company) opened.

Colley Cibber born.

Milton's *Paradise Regained* and *Samson Agonistes* published.

Dryden's *THE CONQUEST OF GRANADA*, Part II.

THE REHEARSAL, by the Duke of Buckingham and others.

Wycherley's *LOVE IN A WOOD*.

1672

Third Dutch War began (ended 1674).

Joseph Addison born.

Richard Steele born.
Dyden's *MARRIAGE A LA MODE.*

1674

New Drury Lane Theatre (King's Company) opened.
Death of Milton.
Thomas Rymer's *Reflections on Aristotle's Treatise of Poesy* (translation of Rapin) published.

Born June 20 at Little Barford, Bedfordshire.

1675

Dryden's *AURENG-ZEBE.*
Wycherley's *THE COUNTRY WIFE.**

1676

Etherege's *THE MAN OF MODE.*
Otway's *DON CARLOS.*
Shadwell's *THE VIRTUOSO.*
Wycherley's *THE PLAIN DEALER.*

1677

Rymer's *Tragedies of the Last Age Considered* published.
Behn's *THE ROVER.*
Dryden's *ALL FOR LOVE.*
Lee's *THE RIVAL QUEENS.*

1678

Popish Plot.
George Farquhar born.
Bunyan's *Pilgrim's Progress* (Part I) published.

1679

Exclusion Bill introduced.
Death of Thomas Hobbes.
Death of Roger Boyle, Earl Of Orrery.
Charles Johnson born.

1680

Death of Samuel Butler.
Death of John Wilmot, Earl Of Rochester.
Dryden's *THE SPANISH FRIAR.*
Lee's *LUCIUS JUNIUS BRUTUS.*
Otway's *THE ORPHAN.*

Education began* at "a private Grammar-School in Highgate."

89

1681

Charles II dissolved Parliament at Oxford.

Dryden's *Absalom and Achitophel* published.

Tate's adaptation of *KING LEAR*.

1682

The King's and the Duke of York's Companies merged into the United Company.

Dryden's *The Medal, MacFlecknoe,* and *Religio Laici* published.

Otway's *VENICE PRESERVED*.

1683

Rye House Plot.

Death of Thomas Killigrew.

Crowne's *CITY POLITIQUES*.

1685

Death of Charles II; accession of James II.

Revocation of the Edict of Nantes.

The Duke of Monmouth's Rebellion.

Death of Otway.

John Gay born.

Crowne's *SIR COURTLY NICE*.

Dryden's *ALBION AND ALBANIUS*.

1687

Death of the Duke of Buckingham.

Dryden's *The Hind and the Panther* published.

Newton's *Principia* published.

1688

The Revolution.

Alexander Pope born.

Shadwell's *THE SQUIRE OF ALSATIA*.

At fourteen* elected a Kings's Scholar at Westminster School.

1689

The War of the League of Augsburg began (ended 1697).

Toleration Act.

Death of Aphra Behn.

Shadwell made Poet Laureate.
Dryden's *DON SEBASTIAN*.
Shadwell's *BURY FAIR*.

1690
Battle of the Boyne.
Locke's *Two Treatises of Government*
and *An Essay Concerning Human
Understanding* published.

1691
Death of Etherege.* Admitted to the Middle Temple
Langbaine's *An Account of the Eng-* August 4.
lish Dramatic Poets published.

1692
Death of Lee. John Rowe (buried May 7)
Death of Shadwell. bequeathed Nicholas £ 300 a year
Tate made Poet Laureate. and his Temple chambers.
1693
George Lillo born*.
Rymer's *A Short View of Tragedy* pub-
lished.
Congreve's *THE OLD BACHELOR*.

1694
Death of Queen Mary.
Southerne's *THE FATAL MAR-
RIAGE*.

1695
Group of actors led by Thomas
Betterton left Drury Lane and
established a new company at Lin-
coln's Inn Fields.
Congreve's *LOVE FOR LOVE*.
Southerne's *OROONOKO*.

1696
Cibber's *LOVE'S LAST SHIFT*. Called to the Bar, May 22.
Vanbrugh's *THE RELAPSE*.

1697
Treaty of Ryswick ended the War
of the League of Augsburg.
Charles Macklin born.
Congreve's *THE MOURNING
BRIDE*.
Vanbrugh's *THE PROVOKED
WIFE*.

91

1698

Collier controversy started with the publication of *A Short View of the Immorality and Profaneness of the English Stage*.

Married Antonia Parsons, daughter of Antony Parsons, auditor of the revenue.

1699

Farquhar's *THE CONSTANT COUPLE*.

Son John born, christened at St. Andrew's, Holborn, August 24.

1700

Death of Dryden.

Blackmore's *Satire against Wit* published.

Congreve's *THE WAY OF THE WORLD*.

THE AMBITIOUS STEPMOTHER produced at Lincoln's Inn Fields, December.

1701

Act of Settlement.

War of the Spanish Succession began (ended 1713).

Death of James II.

Steele's *THE FUNERAL*.

TAMBERLANE produced at Lincoln's Inn Fields, December.

1702

Death of William III; accession of Anne.

The Daily Courant began publication.

Cibber's *SHE WOULD AND SHE WOULD NOT*.

1703

Death of Samuel Pepys.

THE FAIR PENITENT produced at Lincoln's Inn Fields, May.

1704

Capture of Gibraltar; Battle of Blenheim.

Defoe's *The Review* began publication (1704–1713).

Swift's *A Tale of a Tub* and *The Battle of the Books* published.

Cibber's *THE CARELESS HUSBAND*.

THE BITER produced at Lincoln's Inn Fields, December 4.

Edited no. 5 of Dryden's *Poetical Miscellanies*.

1705

Haymarket Theatre opened.

Steele's *THE TENDER HUSBAND*.

ULYSSES produced at the (Queen's) Haymarket Theatre, November 23.

1706

Battle of Ramillies.
Farquhar's *THE RECRUITING OFFICER.*

Death of Rowe's wife, Antonia Parsons Rowe, January 18.

1707

Union of Scotland and England.
Death of Farquhar.
Henry Fielding born.
Farquhar's *THE BEAUX' STRATAGEM.*

THE ROYAL CONVERT produced at the (Queen's) Haymarket Theatre, November 25.
Translation of *The Golden Verses of Pythagoras* and a poem *On the Late Glorious Successes of Her Majesty's Arms* published.

1708

Downes' *Roscius Anglicanus* published.

John Ozell's translation of Boileau's *Lutrin* published with preface by Rowe.
An Original Chapter of the Manner of Living with Great Men, after the Manner of de la Bruyère published.
Press announcement of Rowe's intended edition of the *Works of Mr. William Shakespear,* in *The Daily Courant,* 17 March.

1709

Samuel Johnson born.
The Tatler began publication (1709–1711).
Centlivre's *THE BUSY BODY.*

Appointed Under-Secretary to Duke of Queensberry, 5 February.
The Works of Mr. William Shakespear published in six volumes.
Edited No. 6 of Dryden's *Poetical Miscellanies.*

1710

Charles Gildin produced a seventh volume of *The Works of Mr. William Shakespear* including the poems and Rowe's biographical essay (unauthorized?).

1711

Shaftesbury's *Characteristics* published.
The Spectator began publication (1711–1712).
Pope's *An Essay on Criticism* published.

93

1712

Claudius Quillet's *Callipaedia, or the Art of Getting Beautiful Children* published in translation (first book only by Rowe).

1713

Treaty of Utrecht ended the War of the Spanish Succession.
Addison's *CATO*.

1714

Death of Anne; accession of George I.
Steele became Governor of Drury Lane.
John Rich assumed management of Lincoln's Inn Fields.
Centlivre's *THE WONDER: A WOMAN KEEPS A SECRET*.

THE TRAGEDY OF JANE SHORE produced at Drury Lane Theatre, 2 February.
The Tragedies of Nicholas Rowe published in two volumes.
The Works of Mr. William Shakespear republished in nine volumes.
Edmund Curll issued a pirated edition of Rowe's poems in quarto and *A New Rehearsal, or Bays the Younger* by Charles Gildon.

1715

Jacobite Rebellion.
Death of Tate.
Death of Wycherley.

Appointed Landwaiter (Land Surveyor of the Customs).*
Made Poet Laureate.
THE TRAGEDY OF LADY JANE GRAY produced at Drury Lane Theatre, 20 April
Appointed Clerk of the Prince of Wales' Council.*
Remarried; to Anne, daughter of Joseph Devenish of Buckham, in Dorsetshire.
Appointed Clerk of the Presentations.*

1716

Addison's *THE DRUMMER*.

Ode for the Year 1716.
Assisted Mrs. Centlivre in writing *THE CRUEL GIFT* and supplied the Epilogue, produced at Drury Lane Theatre, 17 December.
Verses upon the Sickness and Recovery of the Right Hon. Robert Walpole published.

1717
David Garrick born.
Cibber's *THE NON-JUROR*.
Gay, Pope, and Arbuthnot's
THREE HOURS AFTER MAR-RIAGE.

Ode for the Year 1717.
Odes to the King.*

1718
Centlivre's *A BOLD STROKE FOR A WIFE*.

Daughter Charlotte born; christened 1 June.
Completed translation of Lucan's *Pharsalia*.
Died 6 December; buried in Westminster Abbey 19 December.

1719
Death of Addison.
Defoe's *Robinson Crusoe* published.
Young's *BUSIRIS, KING OF EGYPT*.

Ode to the Thames for the Year 1719.
His widow granted pension of £40 per annum by the Crown.

1720
South Sea Bubble.
Samuel Foote born.
Steele suspended from the Governorship of Drury Lane (restored 1721).
Little Theatre in the Haymarket opened.
Steele's *The Theatre* (periodical) published.
Hughes's *THE SIEGE OF DAMASCUS*.

The Dramatic Works of Nicholas Rowe published in two volumes.

1721
Walpole became first Minister.

1722
Steele's *THE CONSCIOUS LOVERS*.

1723
Death of Susanna Centlivre.
Death of D'Urfey.

1725
Pope's edition of Shakespeare published.

1726

Death of Jeremy Collier.

Death of Vanbrugh.

Law's *Unlawfulness of Stage Enter-tainments* published.

Swift's *Gulliver's Travels* published.

1727

Death of George I; accession of George II.

Death of Sir Isaac Newton.

Arthur Murphy born.

1728

Pope's *The Dunciad* (first version) published.

Cibber's *THE PROVOKED HUSBAND* (expansion of Van-brugh's fragment *A JOURNEY TO LONDON*).

Gay's *THE BEGGAR'S OPERA*.

1729

Goodman's Fields Theatre opened.

Death of Congreve.

Death of Steele.

Edmund Burke born.

1730

Cibber made Poet Laureate.

Oliver Goldsmith born.

Thomson's *The Seasons* published.

Fielding's *THE AUTHOR'S FARCE*.

Fielding's *TOM THUMB* (revised as *THE TRAGEDY OF TRAGE-DIES*, 1731).

1731

Death of Defoe.

Fielding's *THE GRUB-STREET OPERA*.

Lillo's *THE LONDON MER-CHANT*.

1732

Covent Garden Theatre opened.

Death of Gay.

96

George Colman the elder born.
Fielding's *THE COVENT GARDEN TRAGEDY*.
Fielding's *THE MODERN HUSBAND*.
Charles Johnson's *CAELIA*.

1733

Pope's *An Essay On Man* (Epistles I–III) published (Epistle IV, 1734).

Miscellaneous Works of Nicholas Rowe published in three volumes.

1734

Death of Dennis.
The Prompter began publication (1734–1736).
Theobald's edition of Shakespeare published.
Fielding's *DON QUIXOTE IN ENGLAND*.

1736

Fielding led the "Great Mogul's Company of Comedians" at the Little Theatre in the Haymarket (1736–1737).
Fielding's *PASQUIN*.
Lillo's *FATAL COURIOSITY*.

Plays Written by Nicholas Rowe published.

1737

The Stage Licensing Act.
Dodsley's *THE KING AND THE MILLER OF MANSFIELD*.
Fielding's *THE HISTORICAL REGISTER FOR 1736*.